SCO

SCOTLAND

Other books by Paul Henderson Scott

1707: The Union of Scotland and England (1979)
John Galt (1985)
In Bed with an Elephant (1985)
The Thinking Nation (1989)
Cultural Independence (1989)
Towards Independence: Essays on Scotland (1991)
Andrew Fletcher and the Treaty of Union (1992 and 1994)
Scotland in Europe: A Dialogue with a Sceptical Friend (1992)

Edited
(With A C Davis) *The Age of MacDiarmid* (1980) (Paperback edition 1992)
Sir Walter Scott's The Letters of Malachi Malagrowther (1981)
Andrew Fletcher's United and Separate Parliaments (1982)
(With George Bruce) *A Scottish Postbag* (1986)
(With AC Davis) *Policy for the Arts: A Selection of AdCAS Papers* (1991)
Scotland: A Concise Cultural History (1993)

Contributions to joint volumes in
(*Ed.* J H Alexander and David Hewitt) *Scott and his Influence* (1983)
(*Ed.* M Anderson and L Dominguez) *Cultural Policy in Europe* (1984)
(*Ed.* Douglas Gifford) *The History of Scottish Literature, Vol. 3* (1988)
(*Ed.* Angus Calder) *Byron and Scotland* (1989)
(*Ed.* C J M MacLachlan and D S Robb) *Edwin Muir: Centenary Assessments* (1990)
(*Ed.* Noelle Watson) *Reference Guide to Short Fiction* (1994)

Portrait by Andrew Geddes, A.R.A. Reproduced by permission of the Scottish National Portrait Gallery.

WALTER SCOTT
AND
SCOTLAND

BY
PAUL HENDERSON SCOTT

SALTIRE
SOCIETY

First published 1981 by William Blackwood, Edinburgh
This paperback edition published 1994 by The Saltire Society, 9 Fountain Close,
High Street, Edinburgh EH1 1TF

The publisher acknowledges subsidy from
the Scottish Arts Council towards the
publication of this volume.

A catalogue record for this book is available from
the British Library.

ISBN 0 85411 056 9

Detail from portrait of Sir Walter Scott by Sir William Allan
reproduced in front cover design by permission of the
Scottish National Portrait Gallery.

Designed by Gourlay Graphics, Glasgow

Printed and bound in Great Britain by Bell & Bain Limited

Contents

Introduction

Yet another book about Walter Scott requires a word of explanation, if not apology. Scott himself was one of the most prolific of writers, but he has been outdone, if they are taken together, by his biographers, critics, apologists and detractors. Will we ever reach the point where everything possible has been said about him? Have we not reached it already?

Partly, I write because I share the feeling expressed by John Buchan in the Preface to his admirable *Life of Scott*: 'It is a book which I was bound one day or other to write, for I have had the fortune to be born and bred under the shadow of that great tradition.' Almost literally under the shadow, because like Walter Scott, I was born in Edinburgh and went to the High School and University but, unlike him, I walked almost daily beneath his towering monument.

A set of the Waverley Novels was my first substantial purchase of books when I was about ten years old. Since then, I have continued to read Scott and I have been puzzled by many things about him. To seek answers I have gradually explored the vast literature about him. It is because I have not found satisfactory answers to my questions in any of these books that I am obliged to write my own. Many of the existing books are admirable, but for the most part they deal with different questions.

I am conscious, of course, of the similarity of my title to the one used by Edwin Muir for his celebrated, or notorious, book, published in 1936, *Scott and Scotland: The Predicament of the Scottish Writer*. This is because the aspect of the subject which I want to write about is the one which was given to Muir, but from which he was quickly side-tracked. He explains this with complete honesty on his first page:

> The original intention of this series was that a number of writers should select some figure or subject and inquire what he or it had done for Scotland. The figure allotted to me was Walter Scott. I began to discover what he had done for Scotland, but had scarcely started before I saw that a much more promising subject for inquiry would be what Scotland had done for him. This very quickly led me to consider the position of the writer in Scotland generally, a position which is both unhappy and unique.

Muir really wanted to write about MacDiarmid's use of the Scots language, and the chapter about Scott comes almost as an afterthought towards the end of the book. It is a brilliantly intuitive and provocative piece of writing which stirred up one of the liveliest controversies in the history of Scottish letters; but it had very little to do with Scott himself and I do not have the impression that Muir had read much of Scott or thought much about him.

Muir does raise one of the questions, perhaps the main one, which I want to pursue, the effect on Scott himself of Scotland's loss of independence. It seems clear to me that this was a constant preoccupation of Scott and the emotional force behind much of his work; but it is one which has been largely ignored or even deliberately distorted. This is partly because much of the criticism has been written outside Scotland by writers with very little knowledge of Scottish history and innocent of all awareness of what Muir properly calls 'the Scottish predicament'. Georg Lukàcs, for instance (whose book, *The Historical Novel*, is the fountainhead of most recent criticism of Scott), is capable of the following (unless his translator served him ill): 'it is no accident that this new type of novel arose in England. . . . He [Scott] finds in English history the consolation that the most violent vicissitudes of class struggle have always finally calmed down into a glorious "middle way". Given the very different temper of Scottish history, as different from the English as anything could be, and the fact that Scott's writing is closely involved with the Scottish condition, this is far more than a mere geographical inaccuracy.

Scott, more than almost any other writer, cannot be properly understood without an awareness of the historical position in which he found himself in Scotland, because that is the theme of most of his best work.

My purpose, then, is to attempt to see Scott in this context and to consider what effect it had on his writing and what effect this had in turn on Scotland itself.

1

Scott's Reputation

'The Monarch of Parnassus'

'At this moment, his position, take it for all in all, was, I am inclined to believe, what no other man had ever won for himself by the pen alone.'[1] With these words, Lockhart begins a chapter of his *Life of Scott,* and he is speaking of 1818 when Scott had published only five of his twenty-seven novels and long before he had openly acknowledged any of them. But Lockhart was not exaggerating. It is unusual at any time for a writer to win both popularity and critical approval. Scott won both to an unprecedented degree. Even the narrative poems, such as the *Lay of the Last Minstrel* and *Marmion,* rapidly sold upwards of 50,000 copies. The novels were seized from the press as quickly as they could be printed and soon went through more editions than anyone can easily count. Even before he set doggedly to work to pay off his debts in the last six years of his life, Scott was earning about £10,000 a year from his writing alone. This was at a time when a farm worker was paid about £2 a month and when Scott's salary as Sheriff of Selkirk, considered to be adequate for a life of gentlemanly ease, was £300 annually. The esteem and admiration of the literary world was virtually unanimous. Goethe said he was, 'a great genius who does not have an equal',[2] and that *Waverley* could 'be set beside the best works that have ever been written in this world'. Wordsworth called him, 'this wondrous Potentate',[3] and Southey said that 'no man ever afforded so much delight'.[4] Byron said that he read all the novels at least fifty times[5] and never travelled without them:[6]

Scott is certainly the most wonderful writer of the day. His novels are a new literature in themselves, and his poetry as good as any—if not better[7] . . . He is undoubtedly the Monarch of Parnassus.[8]

Also, Scott's literary influence in other countries was immense. The Hungarian critic, Georg Lukàcs, quotes Pushkin: 'The influence of Walter Scott can be felt in every province of the literature of his age.'[9] Paul Ochojski says that, 'his effect on German literature was incalculable' and quotes Luise Sigmann, 'The popularity of Scott is so great that we may regard him as almost a German writer'.[10] In France, Hugo and Balzac acclaimed his example; for Balzac, he was 'one of the noblest geniuses of modern times'.[11] French translations of the Waverley Novels were said to have reached sales of two million by 1840. In Italy, Manzoni said that, 'if it had not been for Walter Scott it would never have occurred to him to write a novel'.[12] Many other people in many other countries might have said the same. In places as diverse as Hungary and Quebec, the first novels to be written were imitations of Scott. His influence was felt not only on the novel, but in the whole approach to history and the writing of it. He created a fashion for the middle ages with profound effects, for better or worse, on painting and architecture. Mark Twain even blamed him for the American Civil War: 'Sir Walter had so large a hand in making Southern character, as it existed before the war, that he is in great measure responsible for the war.'[13]

Scott's extraordinary literary reputation survived, almost without abatement, for about one hundred years. It was normal to mention him in the same breath as Chaucer, Cervantes or Shakespeare. I give only a few comparatively recent examples. Lord David Cecil: 'He is a very great novelist indeed – and so far from not being serious, touched depths and heights often that most English novelists could never touch at all. . . . Scott's grasp of the essentials of character has a Shakespearean firmness that allows him to shift a figure through every vicissitude of mood and circumstance.'[14] Herbert Grierson: 'The genial, kindly humanity of a Chaucer, a Cervantes, a Scott.'[15] Virginia Woolf: '. . . he is perhaps the last novelist to practise the great, the Shakespearean art, of making people reveal themselves in speech.'[16]

Of course, this adulation could not continue indefinitely in unbroken succession. Generations of school-boys forced to read some of the less successful of his novels, before they were ripe for them, were bound to rebel in the end. (Why were these novels, *Ivanhoe*, *Kenilworth* and the like chosen? Probably because they were not set in Scotland and therefore contained no dialogue in Scots. This dialogue is one of Scott's greatest literary achievements, but it might have been considered corrupting to the school-boy's English prose.) Sometime during the 1920s and '30s, Scott became very unfashionable and was assumed to be unreadable. The romanticism, Toryism and militarism associated with him, and the absence of eroticism, although far from being the whole story, were alien to the spirit of the age. Scott was widely regarded as boring at best and reactionary at worst. For this view, the *locus classicus* is a lecture which E. M. Forster gave at Cambridge in 1927. He said that he did not care for Scott and found it difficult to understand his continued reputation: 'He is seen to have a trivial mind and a heavy style. He cannot construct. He has neither artistic detachment nor passion.'[17] Certainly, much of Scott's English prose could be described as 'heavy', but Forster's other points were perverse.

Whether consciously replying to Forster or not, a whole school of criticism soon appeared to rebut the charge of triviality. It is not so strange as may at first appear that the first of these voices was a Marxist, Georg Lukàcs, whose book, *The Historical Novel*, was written in 1937, although the English translation did not appear until 1962. For Lukàcs, Scott's novels were the demonstration of changing social and economic conditions through the lives of their characters. You might almost say that for Lukàcs Scott was the first, and one of the greatest, of Marxist writers. A strange role, one might think, for the Tory and anti-revolutionary Scott. In fact, although Lukàcs does not seem to have realised it fully, there is a logical consistency and appropriateness in this view. Many of Scott's ideas were formed by the atmosphere of Enlightenment Edinburgh in which he grew up, and the Scottish philosophical historians of that period, particularly Adam Ferguson and Adam Smith, had a direct influence on Marx. The idea of history as a progression from one stage of social and economic development to another was one of the principal themes of eighteenth-century Edinburgh. The ideas of Scott and Marx were nourished by the same source. Scott's indebtedness to the Enlightenment is obvious once it has been pointed out, and it is in fact apparent in his own short autobiography,[18] but it was Duncan Forbes, as recently as 1953, who first emphasised it.[19] There is now a new analysis of Scott's historicism, notably in the work of David Daiches, A. O. J. Cockshut and David Brown,[20] which has established Scott's intellectual reputation on more solid foundations than ever before. David Daiches said in 1975,[21] 'it is only in the last ten years that we have really understood what Scott's novels are about', and he hardly exaggerated, even if Coleridge, Carlyle, Bagehot and others had a pretty fair idea.

This new appreciation of Scott has been directed to the nine novels set in Scotland in the hundred years or so before his birth: *Waverley* (1814), *Guy Mannering* (1815), *The Antiquary* (1816), *Old Mortality* (1816), *Rob Roy* (1817), *The Heart of Midlothian* (1818), *The Bride of Lammermoor* (1819), *A Legend of Montrose* (1819) and *Redgauntlet* (1824). This, give or take one or two, is the canon on which the new criticism has concentrated; it has ignored the poetry and mentioned the other novels only as examples of comparative failure where Scott ventured outside the country and the period which he knew intimately, although sometimes exceptions are made for *The Fortunes of Nigel* (1822) and *The Fair Maid of Perth* (1828). According to this theory, Scott fails, in the words of David Brown, 'when he treats historical situations in which the class-relationship familiar to his imagination has not come into being, and to which he could not, therefore, apply himself with any confidence of success'.[22] This theory is certainly persuasive, but there may be other reasons for the success of the nine novels, which are certainly the best by any standards. Lord David Cecil, for example, makes a similar selection for reasons which have nothing to do with theories about Scott's historical methods.[23] For one thing, they were all written (as were some of the others) before the financial disaster of 1826 made Scott feel that he had to churn out best-sellers at the greatest possible speed, when masterpieces were hardly to be expected. The novels are also those which gave Scott the best opportunities to deploy his genius for Scottish character and dialogue in Scots. Whatever the reasons, almost everyone would now agree that Scott is at his best when on his native heath. It is true that *Ivanhoe* (1820) in Scott's own time sold best of all his novels, outside Scotland at least, and that *Quentin Durward* (1823) added greatly to his popularity in France, but if he had written nothing but

4

these excursions into the Middle Ages, he would now be remembered only as a writer who provoked an unfortunate fashion for the Gothic.

There are some signs that appreciation of Scott is once again widening beyond the nine novels. As I am writing this, a book, *The Laird of Abbotsford: A View of Sir Walter Scott* by A. N. Wilson, has just appeared. This is full of infectious enthusiasm for a wide range of Scott's writing. He includes the verse, not only the great lyrics but also the narrative poems, to which he turns 'again and again with renewed refreshment and pleasure'.[24] He finds merit even in *Anne of Geierstein*, which first made him 'an addict of the Waverley Novels'.[25] In other respects, it is true, he follows in the tradition of the Lukàcs school, finding, for example, that '*Redgauntlet* is not only a great novel, but a monument in the history of ideas'.[26]

So far, I have been sketching, in the briefest outline, the vicissitudes of Scott's popularity and critical standing as a writer, mainly since Scott's own time and mainly outside Scotland. In the passage from Lockhart's *Life* with which I started, 'his position . . . was . . . what no other man had ever won for himself by the pen alone', Lockhart was thinking not so much of these things as of some effects of them. He goes on to say that Scott 'was courted by whatever England could show of eminence. Station, power, wealth, beauty, and genius, strove with each other in every demonstration of respect and worship'. But there was a special quality of response in Scotland: 'whoever had Scottish blood in him, "gentle or simple", felt it move more rapidly through his veins when he was in the presence of Scott.'[27] There is plenty of evidence in the pages of Lockhart and elsewhere for the truth of these two propositions. Wherever Scott went, he was courted and lionised. When he visited Dublin, Scott himself said that he was treated 'as if I was a Prince of the Blood'.[28] He might have said the same in London or Paris. In Scotland itself, his position was unique; he was not so much the 'Monarch of Parnassus', as the dominant figure in the entire life of the country, to an extent which it is difficult to describe without seeming to exaggerate. There was a well-known episode close to the end of Scott's life when his opposition to the Reform Bill involved him with a hostile mob, but in general the normal mood was one of enthusiasm and affection. There is a parallel in the adulation of Burns since his death, but Scott was a national hero in his own life time.

When Sir Robert Peel was in Edinburgh in August 1822, during the visit of George IV, he walked with Scott along the High Street. He described the episode in a speech some years later: 'He was recognised from one extremity of the street to the other, and never did I see such an instance of national devotion.'[29] It was this, he said, which first gave him a notion of the 'electric shock of a nation's gratitude'.[30] The same word, gratitude, was repeated in Lord Meadowbank's speech at a public dinner in the Assembly Rooms in Edinburgh on the 23rd February 1826, when Scott openly acknowledged for the first time that he had written the Waverley Novels: 'We owe to him, as a people, a large and heavy debt of gratitude.'[31] Henry Cockburn struck the same note. On 22nd September 1832, the day after Scott's death, he wrote in his *Journal*: 'Scotland never owed so much to one man.'[32]

If Scott's main work is in these nine Scottish novels and if the secret of who had written them was kept until 1826, one might well wonder what had provoked this sense of national gratitude as early as 1822. There are, I think, two explanations. In the first place, the secret was very transparent and really existed only in the mind of Scott himself. As David Daiches has recently reminded us,[33] the personality of Walter Scott was written clearly over every page of the Scottish novels: his favourite phrases, his favourite anecdotes, all the habitual turns and habits of his conversation were obvious to anyone who knew him, even to those who only knew him by his writing. In 1821 J. L. Adolphus, then an undergraduate at Oxford, in his *Letter to Richard Heber,* proved on internal evidence alone that the author of the novels must be the same man that had written the *Lay of the Last Minstrel* and *Marmion.* Even earlier, in fact only just over two months after the publication of *Waverley*, the first of the novels, Jane Austen wrote this in a letter to her niece, Anna on 28th September 1814:

> Walter Scott has no business to write novels, especially good ones. – It is not fair. – He has Fame and Profit enough as a Poet, and should not be taking the bread out of other people's mouths. – I do not like him, and do not mean to like *Waverley* if I can help it – but I fear I must.[34]

In Germany, the translations of the novels from 1823 onwards were published under the name of Walter Scott without prevarication.[35] When Scott was in Dublin in 1824, one of the Trinity College librarians said to Scott, 'I have been so busy that I have not yet read your *Redgauntlet*'. He replied, 'I have not happened to fall in with such a work, Doctor';[36] but it is unlikely if the librarian, or anyone else, was deceived by the mystification which it pleased Scott to keep up. If Jane Austen, deep in the countryside of the South of England, remote from the literary gossip of both London and Edinburgh, knew who had written *Waverley*, it is impossible to imagine that Scott's own countrymen had any doubts.

Secondly, Scott's position, in Scotland at least, was not due to his writing alone. It was partly that his devotion to the country and its people was so strong and so obvious. 'The love of his country became indeed a passion', says Lockhart in the Conclusion of his *Life*; 'he would have bled and died to preserve even the airiest surviving nothing of her antique pretensions for Scotland'.[37] Or as his friend, James Skene expressed it, 'there did not breathe a man within these Kingdoms so disinterestedly and intensely patriotic as Sir Walter Scott, in so far as patriotism consists in the love of and devotion to one's country, in anxiety for its best interests, and pure affection for one's countrymen'.[38] These feelings were apparent in his dealings with all manner of people 'with such ease and unaffected simplicity as never, perhaps was seen before in any man so gifted', as Captain Hall recorded.[39] Or, as a worker at Abbotsford put it more simply, 'Sir Walter speaks to every man as if they were blood-relations'.[40] Testimony to his modest, unassuming behaviour, to his warm humanity, to his sheer decency and goodness are legion, but perhaps one of the most eloquent is Byron's in a letter to Stendhal on 29th May 1823:

> I have known Walter Scott long and well, and in occasional situations which call forth the *real* character – and I can assure you that his character *is* worthy of admiration – that of all men he is the most *open*, the most *honourable*, the most *amiable*. With his politics I have nothing to do; they differ from mine, which renders it difficult for me to speak of them. But he is *perfectly sincere* in them . . . *believe* the *truth*. I say that Walter Scott is as nearly a thorough good man as man can be, because I *know* it by experience to be the case.[41]

But does any of this explain why Peel, Meadowbank and Cockburn speak so emphatically of 'a nation's gratitude'? This is, after all, a somewhat unusual response to the work of a writer.

7

Meadowbank in his speech offered some explanation in a passage which, making due allowance for after-dinner rhetoric on an emotional occasion, raises a number of questions. (What, for example, does he mean in the context by 'that independence and that liberty'?):

> He it is who has opened to foreigners the grand and characteristic beauties of our country. It is to him that we owe that our gallant ancestors and illustrious patriots – who fought and bled in order to obtain and secure that independence and that liberty we now enjoy – have obtained a fame no longer confined to the boundaries of a remote and comparatively obscure country – it is *He* who has called down upon their struggles for glory and freedom the admiration of foreign lands. He it is who has conferred a new reputation on our national character, and bestowed on Scotland an imperishable name, were it only by her having given birth to himself.[42]

This whole idea of national gratitude comes close to the heart of the questions of what Scott had done for Scotland and what Scotland had done for him. Before attempting any answers, I should like to look first at some of the apparent contradictions in Scott's attitudes and then try to see to what extent they follow from the circumstances in which he grew up.

NOTES

Chapter quotation: Byron, *Letters and Journals*, Ed. by Leslie A. Marchand, Vol. III, p. 219.

[1] **Lockhart, J. G.,** *Life* (Edn of 1900), Vol. III, Chapter XLI, p. 180.

[2] Quoted *Scott Bicentenary Essays*, Ed. by Alan Bell (Edinburgh and London, 1973), pp. 260 and 265.

[3] **Wordsworth, W.,** *Yarrow Revisited* (Oxford Standard Authors), p. 387, line 12.

[4] **Southey, R.,** in a letter to Scott, quoted in Lockhart's *Life*, Vol. III, Chapter XLIV, p. 262.

[5] **Byron, Lord,** *Letters and Journals,* Ed. by Leslie A. Marchand, Vol. 8, p. 13 (11 Vols., London, 1973-81).

[6] ibid, Vol. 9, p. 87.

[7] ibid, Vol. 8, p. 23.

[8] ibid, Vol. 3, p. 219.

[9] **Lukàcs, G.,** p. 31.

[10] *Bicentenary Essays,* p. 260.

[11] *Scott: The Critical Heritage,* p. 374.

[12] Quoted *Bicentenary Essays,* p. 295.

[13] *The Critical Heritage,* Ed. by John O. Hayden (London, 1970), p. 538.

[14] **Cecil, Lord David,** *Sir Walter Scott,* p. 29 (1933).

[15] *Sir Walter Scott Lectures 1940-48,* Ed. by W. I. Renwick, p. 51 (1950).

[16] **Woolf, Virginia,** *Sir Walter Scott* (1924) in *Collected Essays,* p. 143 (1966).

[17] **Forster, E. M.:** *Aspects of the Novel* (1927), Penguin Books edition, p. 38 (1962).

[18] This is prefixed to Lockhart's *Life,* e.g. in edition of 1900, Vol. I, pp. 1–47.

[19] **Forbes, Duncan,** 'The Rationalism of Sir Walter Scott' in *The Cambridge Journal* (Oct. 1953), Vol. VII, pp. 20–35.

[20] **Daiches, David,** *Scott's Achievement as a Novelist in Literary Essays* (1956).
Cockshut, A. O. J., *The Achievement of Walter Scott* (1969).
Brown, David, *Walter Scott and the Historical Imagination* (1979).

[21] In a lecture at a Saltire Society Conference in St Andrews, September 1975.

[22] **Brown, David,** op cit, p. 184.

[23] **Cecil, Lord David,** *Sir Walter Scott,* p. 10 (1933).

[24] op cit, p. 23.

[25] ibid, pp. 159–60.

[26] ibid, p. 76.

[27] **Lockhart, J. G.,** *Life,* Vol. III, Chapter XLI, p. 180.

[28] ibid, Vol. IV, Chapter LXIII, p. 291.

[29] ibid, Vol. IV, Chapter LVI, p. 43.

[30] ibid, Vol. IV, Chapter LXIII, p. 288.

[31] ibid, Vol. V, Chapter LXXIII, p. 93.

[32] **Cockburn, Henry,** *Journal 1831-1854,* edition of 1874, Vol. I, p. 37.

[33] In his essay, 'Scott's *Waverley*: The Presence of the Author' in *Nineteenth-Century Scottish Fiction,* Ed. by Ian Campbell, pp. 6–17 (1979).

[34] *The Critical Heritage,* p. 74.

[35] **Ochojski, Paul M.,** in *Bicentenary Essays,* p. 261.

[36] **Lockhart, J. G.,** *Life,* Vol. IV, Chapter LXIII, p. 291.

[37] ibid, Vol. V, Chapter LXXXIV, p. 435.

[38] **Skene, James,** *Memories of Sir Walter Scott,* Ed. by Basil Thomson, pp. 212–13 (1909).

[39] **Lockhart, J. G.,** *Life,* Vol. IV, Chapter LXI, p. 218.

[40] ibid, Vol. IV, Chapter LX, p. 147.

[41] **Byron, Lord,** *Letters and Journals,* Vol. 10, pp. 189–90.

[42] As 31 above.

2

Combination of Opposites

'We need not be surprised to find that in his literature the Scot presents two aspects which appear contradictory.'

Since Gregory Smith invented the term, the 'Caledonian antisyzygy',[1] and particularly since it was taken up by Hugh MacDiarmid, no description of any Scotsman seems to be complete without a reference to it. It was, Smith said, a 'combination of opposites' which was to be found at every turn in Scottish character, history and literature. Certainly it would be easy to discuss Scott in these terms. He, indeed, anticipated Gregory Smith. 'The Scottish Mind', he told Washington Irving, 'was made up of poetry and strong common sense; and the very strength of the latter gave perpetuity and luxuriance to the former'.[2] This is not a bad description of Scott himself. He was an inspiration to the romantic movement all over Europe, but he had no patience with the romantic self-indulgence of the personality. He was robustly sane and devoted to the stoicism and Roman *Severitas*[3] which is so strong a strain in the Scottish character. 'I am a bad comforter in case of inevitable calamity; and feeling proudly able to endure in my own case, I cannot sympathise with those whose nerves are of a feeble texture,' he wrote in his *Journal* on 3rd February 1827 when he was enduring the death of his wife and the collapse of his fortune. Or, on 22nd June 1826, even closer to those events, 'my feelings are rather guided by reflection than impulse. But everybody has his own mode of expressing interest, and mine is stoical even in bitterest grief. *Agere atque pati Romanum est'*.

Scott was delighted with Byron's remark to Moore, 'damn me,

Tom, don't be poetical'.[4] In this same sense of the word, Scott was the least poetical of poets and the least pretentious of writers. In the 1830 Introduction to the *Lady of the Lake*, he said that he had never been a partisan of his own poetry. His daughter, Sophia, said that she had never read it, because 'Papa says there's nothing so bad for young people as reading bad poetry'.[5] When it was suggested to him that the Duke of Wellington would receive him as a great poet and novelist, he smiled and said 'What would the Duke of Wellington think of a *few bits of novels*, which perhaps he had never read, and for which the strong possibility is that he would not care a sixpence if he had?'[6] In the Ashestiel fragment of autobiography, he described his voracious appetite in his youth for poetry and romances dealing with chivalry, knight-errantry and the like; but, he adds, 'I really believe I have read as much nonsense of this class as any man now living'.[7] It was clearly of this same reading 'without much discrimination' that he was thinking when he wrote in his *Journal* on 18th December 1825, the day when his financial calamity became certain, 'What a life mine has been! – half educated, almost wholly neglected or left to myself, stuffing my head with the most nonsensical trash'.[8] For the purposes of his argument, Edwin Muir chooses to regard the 'nonsensical trash' as the 'scattered fragments of Scotland's past which he brooded over in his mind while he watched the Scottish tradition vanishing'.[9] If he had read the Ashestiel *Memoir* (and he seems to have read only John Buchan's *Life* for his biographical information), he would have seen that Scott's meaning was plain enough. Scott is full of regret that his education had not been more rigorous and systematic, although it was arduous and thorough enough by most standards, and he deplores his own indulgence in the romantic. He told Wordsworth in a letter that he had written *The Lay of the Last Minstrel*, 'for no other reason than to discharge my mind of the ideas which from infancy have rushed upon it'. He had 'thus expelled from my brain the Fiend of Chivalry'.[10]

Always with Scott's remarks about himself, allowances have to be made for his habit of self-denigration. In his *Journal*, for instance, he often admits to indolence. 'My indolence, if I call it so, is of a capricious kind. It never makes me absolutely idle, but very often inclines me – as it were from more contradictions' sake – to exchange the task of the day for something which I am not obliged to do at the moment, and perhaps not at all.'[11] This was the indolence of a man who held two legal appointments, lived the life of a country gentleman, entertained a flood of visitors, sat on boards and committees and somehow found time to write twenty-six novels, a large volume of verse, thirty-two of miscellaneous prose, thousands of letters which fill twelve further volumes, as well as editing Swift and Dryden, and so forth. Scott was 'half educated' in the same way that he was 'indolent', by his own standards only.

There are those who would deny that Scott was a romantic at all. Boris Ford, for instance: 'He was no romantic; he was an Augustan, who brought to bear on romantic materials a mind humorous and wordly-wise, extrovert and sane.'[12] Edgar Johnson, who brought a life-time's study of Scott to his meticulous biography, says that the romanticism of Scott is an 'exploded notion'. . . . 'Romanticism is a state of feeling, not a body of subject matter. . . . Certainly Scott, like almost all of us, had a romantic strain, but the fundamental nature of his mind and feeling was realistic, rationalistic, and stoic.'[13] David Brown discusses the novels in terms of the melodramatic, romantic, supernatural elements as the 'external paraphernalia' of the conventional novel of Scott's time superimposed on a realistic description of the social, political and economic situation out of which the events or the characters grew. For Brown, as for most contemporary critics, it is the realism which matters.[14] My own preference is the same. In the novels the romantic apparatus is often something we have to tolerate for the sake of the rest. But can we deny that the romantic elements do not also exist or sometimes take over completely? To ignore or deny the romanticism altogether is going from one extreme to the other. Whether Scott was a natural romantic, disciplined by the attitudes of Enlightenment Edinburgh, or a natural rationalist, seduced by the fashion for the romantic, both attitudes exist together.

The romantic apparatus includes, of course, the supernatural in the shape of apparitions, omens, predictions, curses and the like. Sometimes this can be tiresome and absurd enough, but it also leads to some of the great scenes like Meg Merrilees' diatribe against Ellangowan and haunting lyrics like 'Proud Maisie'. 'Wandering Willie's Tale' in *Redgauntlet*, one of the supreme heights – perhaps the finest thing in all prose in Scots – is about a descent into Hell, so vivid that it almost suspends disbelief. In *The Bride of Lammermoor*, the continuous supernatural overtones are not only an integral part of the total effect, but essential to the motivation of the characters. The supernatural is not all dross. After all, Scott did not have to follow the example of the Gothic novelists; he did it quite consciously and deliberately because he enjoyed it. If he was an enlightened sceptic, he also had a life-long enthusiasm for the subject, as may be seen in his *Letters on Demonology and Witchcraft*. In his essay on Horace Walpole he talks about 'that secret and reserved feeling of love for the marvellous and supernatural, which occupies a hidden corner in almost every bosom'.[15] He goes on to say: 'Romantic narrative is of two minds – that which, being in itself possible, may be a matter of belief at any period; and that which, though held impossible by more enlightened ages, was yet consonant with the faith of earlier times.'[16] Here we have together the two key words, romantic and enlightened; Scott blended the two attitudes in his use of the supernatural. He exploited the romantic effect, and either left open the possibility of a rational explanation or explored the psychological effects on people who really believed. In this, as in other matters, the romantic and the man of the Enlightenment were working hand in hand.

Scott himself uses the word 'romantic' quite frequently. In the Ashesteil *Memoir*, he so describes his chivalric reading and the feelings which landscape aroused in him, especially when it was associated with legend or history. In the novels, he often uses the word interchangeably with 'picturesque' to describe scenery. An example from *A Legend of Montrose*:

> In present times, a scene so romantic would have been judged to possess the highest charms for the traveller; but those who journey in days of doubt and dread, pay little attention to picturesque scenery.[17]

In the last chapter of *Waverley*, 'A Postscript which should have been a Preface', he says, 'the most romantic parts of this narrative are precisely those which have a foundation in fact'. He goes on to give examples of what he means: 'The exchange of mutual protection between a Highland gentleman and an officer of rank in the King's service . . . strange concealments, and wild and hair's breadth "scapes" and so forth.'[18] In other words, anything improbable, impracticable, adventurous or out of the way of everyday life is 'romantic'. Elsewhere, the word seems to mean the opposite of mercenary, to apply to the traditional virtues of agricultural society which not only Scott but the philosophers of the Scottish Enlightenment saw as disappearing under pressures of commercialism. Again in *The Legend of Montrose*, Scott speaks of 'the generous, romantic, disinterested chivalry of the old heroic times, entirely different from the sordid, calculating, and selfish character, which the practice of entertaining mercenary troops had introduced into most parts of Europe'.[19] Later in the same novel, he seems almost to be using the word in a more modern sense, when he makes Montrose say 'this poor girl is exquisitely beautiful, and has talents formed to captivate your romantic temper';[20] but he probably again means generous and unrealistic. Perhaps these meanings come together when he speaks of this same girl, Annot Lyle, having a 'romantic plan . . . of nursing in secret her pensive tenderness',[21] in romantic love with Williamina Belsches all his life, romantic in the original sense because his love was unrealised and unobtainable. If to be interested in, and approve of, the attitudes which Scott describes with this vague and diverse word is to be a romantic, then that is certainly an essential part of him.

Lockhart uses the same over-worked word to introduce a discussion of another of the contradictions, Scott's attitude to class. 'The whole system of conceptions and aspirations, of which his early active life was the exponent, resolves itself into a romantic idealisation of Scottish aristocracy.'[22] Or on an earlier page, 'His imagination had been constantly exercised in recalling and embellishing whatever features of the past it was possible to connect with any pleasing ideas, and a historical name was a charm that literally stirred his blood. But not so a mere title.'[23] James Hogg, from a very different social background from Lockhart, made the same point but missed the distinction between name and title:

> The only foible I ever could discover in the character of Sir Walter was a too strong leaning to the old aristocracy of the country. His devotion for titled rank was prodigious and in such an illustrious character altogether out of place. It amounted almost to adoration.[24]

For someone with Scott's passionate concern with the Scottish past, this is an eccentricity perhaps, but it is comprehensible. The feudal history of Scotland revolves round a few prominent families. The fact that their descendants with the same name or title still existed in the contemporary world was a sign of continuity with the past. Scott was deeply concerned with that continuity; it can be seen

14

as a theme of much of his writing. I think that it is possible to imagine how he felt, and even to sympathise with his feelings, when he met a living representative of one of the chief actors in that past which occupied his intellect and stimulated his imagination. But I also think that Lockhart was right in describing this as a 'romantic idealisation'. Scott knew very well, and often made it clear in his writing quite bluntly, that most of these families at one time or another, if not most of the time, had behaved abominably. Read, for example, his account in *The Tales of a Grandfather* of the way in which the Scottish Commissioners, most of them bearers of these same historical names, were brought to accept the terms of the Union of the Parliaments in 1707. 'When they united with the degradation of their country the prospect of obtaining personal wealth and private emoluments, we cannot acquit them of the charge of having sold their own honour and that of Scotland.'[25] His attitude to this aristocracy was another instance of the conflict within Scott's romantic imagination and his practical common sense.

His contradiction over class did not end with this. He accepted without much question the social conventions of his time according to which everyone was more or less firmly placed at birth in a class hierarchy and where there was a deep gulf fixed between 'gentlemen' and the others. His Ashesteil *Memoir* begins and ends with a deference to it. There are the famous words in the third paragraph: 'Every Scottishman has a pedigree. It is a national prerogative as unalienable as his pride and his poverty. My birth was neither distinguished nor sordid.' And ends with these: 'I was a gentleman, and so welcome anywhere, if so be I could behave myself, as Tony Lumpkin says, "in a concatenation accordingly".'[26] Of course, almost everyone else in his day also accepted such notions as facts of life; but in contradiction with both the convention and the romantic attitude to the aristocracy, Scott was in practice a thorough-going egalitarian. Possibly this was, and is, easier in Scotland than in some other places; it is part of the tradition; but Scott carried it much further than most people. Even Lockhart, who was a bit of a snob, seems to approve, and says that Scott got far more pleasure from the friendship of ordinary men and women than from the 'great world' which courted him.[27] Among his innumerable friends of all kinds and conditions, Scott seems to have enjoyed most the company of Tom Purdie, the reformed poacher.[28]

There is a revealing episode in the *Life* where Lockhart tells a story against himself:

> I happened to use some phrase which conveyed (though not perhaps meant to do so) the impression that I suspected poets and novelists of being a good deal accustomed to look at life and the world only as materials for art. A soft and pensive shade came over Scott's face as he said – "I fear you have some very young ideas in your head; – are you not too apt to measure things by some reference to literature – to disbelieve that anybody can be worth much care who has no knowledge of that sort of thing, or taste for it? God help us! What a poor world this would be if that were the true doctrine! I have read books enough, and observed and conversed with enough of eminent and splendidly cultivated minds, too, in my time; but I assure you, I have heard higher sentiments from the lips of poor *uneducated* men and women, when exerting the spirit of severe yet gentle heroism under difficulties and afflictions, or speaking their simple thoughts as to circumstances in the lot of friends or neighbours, than I ever met with out of the pages of the Bible."[29]

Scott's novels are entirely consistent with this view of life.

As Edwin Muir put it, Scott's characters are 'half flesh and blood and half pasteboard, unreal where he dealt with highly civilised people, and real where he dealt with peasants, adventurers and beggars'.[30] Scott's contemporary, Sydney Smith, said in a letter to Constable, 'Sir Walter, always fails in well bred men and women, – and yet, who has seen more of both and who in the ordinary intercourse of society is better bred?'[31] They were both exaggerating, because the social range of Scott's rounded and convincing characters is very wide, including for instance King James VI in *The Fortunes of Nigel*, and the prosperous, Glasgow bourgeois, Baillie Nicol Jarvie in *Rob Roy* (two of the finest) as well as the peasant and the beggars. The lawyers, Pleydell in *Guy Mannering* and Saunders Fairford in *Redgauntlet* are civilised enough, but they are as real as any. It is true that nearly all the great characters speak Scots, but that does not mean that they are therefore peasants or uncivilised. Still Muir and Smith have a real point. Most of Scott's best characters are simple people. They are not there, as in most literature before Scott's time for ridicule, light relief or low comedy like Bottom and the 'hard-handed men' in *A Mid-Summer Night's Dream*; they are as diverse as life, but they often rise to a greatness of

16

action or comment, even to real grandeur or poetry, before which the lords and gentlemen are pasteboard indeed. Jeanie Deans is a simple peasant girl, if you like, but few heroines in literature rise to such heights. Edie Ochiltree is a beggar, but he stands out among all the people in *The Antiquary* for his reliability and common sense. The most heroic figure in *Waverley* is not the Prince or any of the chiefs or officers and gentlemen, but the simple highlander, Evan Maccombich. Meg Merrilees, the outcast gipsy, is capable of devastating eloquence.

Not least of the changes which Scott brought to literature, and to our understanding of history, was his introduction of ordinary people with human dignity and value, splendid and outrageous, comic and serious, but unquestionably alive and playing a serious role in the events of the story. The romantic aristocrat who distrusted democracy was also in a real sense the first of the literary democrats. Scott often depicts aristocratic or gentlemanly behaviour towards social inferiors as arrogant, over-bearing and insufferably rude. Ravenswood in *The Bride of Lammermoor* uses language like 'what do you want, you dog?' or 'Speak out, you old fool'[32] to his old servant Caleb Balderston, whose one desire was to serve him. Scott ridicules characters, like Lady Bellenden or Sir Arthur Wardour, who share his own fondness for ancient family. Sometimes the long-suffering retainers are given a chance to speak back. The same Ravenswood, for instance, for whom our sympathy is enlisted as the dispossessed bearer of an ancient name and representative of the traditional qualities, has an encounter with an old follower of the family now reduced to poverty with the decay of their fortunes:

'If Lord Ravenswood protected his people, my friend, while he had the means of doing so, I think they might share his memory,' replied the master.

'Ye are welcome to your ain opinion, Sir,' said the sexton; 'but ye winna persuade me that he did his duty, either to himself or to huz puir dependant creatures in guiding us the gate he has done – he might hae gien us life rent tacks of our bits o' houses and yards – and me, that's an auld man, living in yon miserable cabin, that's fitter for the dead than the quick, and killed wi' rheumatise, and John Smith in my dainty bit mailing, and his window glazen, and a' because Ravenswood guided his gear like a fule!

'It is but too true,' said Ravenswood, conscience-struck.[33]

17

It was not only in this matter that Scott was given to satirising impulses or characteristics that he knew were his own. Monkbarns in *The Antiquary* was a self-portrait of his own antiquarianism:

A large old-fashioned oak-table was covered with a profusion of papers, parchments, books, and nondescript trinkets and gewgaws, which seemed to have little to recommend them besides rust and the antiquity which it indicates.[34]

The room is Monkbarns's, but it might be a description of Scott's own study. In his essay on Horace Walpole, Scott ridicules the contemporary taste for the Gothic in architecture: 'The Gothic order of architecture is now so generally, and, indeed, indiscriminately used, that we are rather surprised if the country-house of a tradesman retired from business does not exhibit lanceolated windows, divided by stone shafts, and garnished by painted glass, a cupboard in the form of a cathedral stall, and a pig-house with a front borrowed from the facade of an ancient chapel.'[35] One thinks at once of Abbotsford, which probably did more than any other example to encourage precisely the style which he is mocking. At the same time, Scott loved the house, spent great effort and thought on the design and building as well as the borrowed money which caused his financial disaster.

Abbotsford was not only Gothic and filled with nondescript trinkets and gewgaws, it was also one of the first houses to be lit by gas and had a new system of pneumatic bells. Scott in Virginia Woolf's phrase was 'the last minstrel and the first chairman of the Edinburgh oil gas company'.[36] He had both a romantic enthusiasm for any relic of the past and a boyish delight in the latest technology.

The contrast between the romantic and the realist is especially apparent in Scott's attitude to violence and war. He often said in his letters that he would rather have been a soldier than anything else. To Lady Abercorn in 1811, for instance, 'my heart is a soldier's, and always has been, though my lameness rendered me unfit for the profession, which, old as I am, I would rather follow than any other. But these are waking dreams, in which I seldom indulge even to my kindest friends'.[37] He says of his service as Quartermaster of the Edinburgh Light-Horse during the invasion scare of 1796-97 that it 'occupied many of the happiest hours of my life'.[38] He described himself in a letter of 1805: 'You would expect to see a person who

18

had dedicated himself much to literary pursuits, and you would find me a rattle-skulled half-lawyer, half-sportsman, through whose head a regiment of horse has been exercising since he was five years old; half-educated – half-crazy, as his friends sometimes tell him; half-everything.'[39] When ill-health kept him in bed in his days as a legal apprentice, he had fought his way through military histories 'by the childish expedient of arranging shells, and seeds, and pebbles, so as to represent encountering armies'.[40] From his earliest years he had been fascinated both by the tactics and technique of war and by romantic ideas of the panache, glory and courage of it. Even if he defied his lameness, he had the cripple's need to seek compensation in an imaginary life of action. The novels are full of it and his description of battles is magnificent. But at the same time, Scott was fully conscious of the futility and waste of war, and always in favour of peace and stability. Like Saunders Fairford in *Redgauntlet* (who was based on his own father) Scott believed that the time had come for civil rather than military courage.[41]

Of this the most striking demonstration is in the *Letters of Malachi Malagrowther* (1826). Scott had seized a chance to speak out against what he called the English tendency to assume 'the management of affairs entirely and exclusively proper to Scotland, as if it were totally unworthy of having the management of our own concerns'.[42] It was a passionate defence of Scottish rights and of Scottish identity. 'I am certainly serious in *Malachi* if seriousness will do good,' he wrote to James Ballantyne: 'I will sleep quieter in my grave for having so fair an opportunity of speaking my mind.'[43] But even in this controversial mood, all his national feeling aroused, Scott was careful to argue against violence. That would be a retrograde step and rather than that, 'we had better remain in union with England, even at the risk of becoming a subordinate species of Northumberland, as far as national consequence is concerned'.[44] Since the whole purpose of the pamphlet is to argue for the precise opposite of such an outcome, Scott could not have given a clearer proof that he hated the thought of any resort to force.

What then of Scott who was an enthusiastic supporter of the war against Napoleon and was ready to leap into the saddle to suppress discontented weavers, coal-miners and radicals? In all of this, whether we agree with him or not, his attitude was defensive. He can be condemned as an excitable reactionary, but he grew to

19

maturity during the French Revolution and was therefore disposed to see threats of the violent overthrow of society, which it is easy to see in retrospect as exaggerated. He did not seek to provoke violence, but to prevent it.

One of the most discussed of the 'combination of opposites' in Scott is his attitude to Jacobitism, naturally because he thought a great deal about it and made it the subject of three of his best novels, *Waverley, Rob Roy* and *Redgauntlet*. He described his feelings about it in a letter of 17th December 1806 to Robert Surtees:

> The truth is that the subject has often and deeply interested me from my earliest youth. My great-grandfather was *out*, as the phrase goes, in Dundee's wars and in 1715, and had nearly the honour to be hanged for his pains. . . . But besides this, my father, although a Borderer, transacted business for my Highland lairds, and particularly for one old man called Stuart of Invernahyle, who had been out both in 1715 and '45, and whose tales were the absolute delight of my childhood. . . . I became a violent Jacobite at the age of 10 years, and ever since reason and reading came to my assistance, I have never quite got rid of the impression which the gallantry of Prince Charles made on my imagination.[45]

Of course 'reason and reading' did modify his youthful enthusiasm. There is a more judicious summing-up of his adult position in a letter to Miss Clephane in July 1813, 'I am very glad I did not live in 1745 for though as a lawyer I could not have pleaded Charles's right and as a clergyman I could not have prayed for him yet as a soldier I would I am sure against the conviction of my better reason have fought for him even to the bottom of the gallows'.[46] On 14th July 1828 he wrote to Lockhart about Robert Burns, 'his Jacobitism, like my own, belonged to the fancy rather than the reason'.[47] (In the same letter, incidentally, he said that he would not write a Life of Mary, Queen of Scots, 'because my opinion, in point of fact, is contrary both to the popular feeling and to my own'.) Clearly Scott was fully conscious of these conflicts between his feelings and his reason. In a book review in 1809 he spoke of Jacobitism in terms which balances his rational opposition to it against its romantic appeal: 'The side of Charles Edward was the party, not surely of sound sense and sober reason, but of romantic gallantry and high achievement . . . calculated to impress upon the mind of a poet (he is again referring to Burns) a warm interest in the cause of the House of Stuart'.[48] It was the pull of these two contrary impulses which gave both emotional depth and intellectual subtlety to his three Jacobite novels.

Jacobitism in its day and age was neither trivial nor ridiculous. It was bound up intricately with fundamental political, social and religious issues and with ideas about the status of Scotland. There was much about it, apart from the romanticism and gallantry, which appealed to Scott. (For these reasons, I shall return to it later.) At the same time, he knew as well as anyone that it had long been a dead issue. He after all wrote its epitaph in *Redgauntlet*, 'the cause is lost forever'.[49] It is, therefore, absurd to criticise him, as some do, as though he were hypocritical and insincere in not trying to carry on the struggle in his own day.[50] It is perfectly true that he stage-managed the visit of George IV to Scotland in 1822 (the first by a reigning monarch since Charles II) as a sort of act of reconciliation with the Hanoverians. Scott received him almost as one monarch to another, which shows the extraordinary position which he held in Scotland. Of course, there were elements of absurdity and play-acting and probably more tartan in Edinburgh than there had been in 1745; but, the absurdity really derives from the gap between the continuing pretensions of monarchy and the political realities, and from the incongruity between the appearance and personality of the monarch and the role that he was playing. Dynastic questions had lost any real meaning and become a sort of harmless pageant.

If Jacobitism was a dead issue, the effects of the Union on Scotland, the creeping anglicisation, were not. In fact they only began to be felt from about the beginning of the nineteenth century. In the eighteenth century, Scotland had been ignored by London and had not only prospered but had reached a great peak of intellectual achievement. But, said Scott, writing in 1826, 'when I look back on the last fifteen or twenty years, and more especially on the last ten, I think I see my native country of Scotland, if it is yet to be called by a title so discriminative, falling, so far as its national, or rather, perhaps, I ought now to say its *provincial* interests are concerned, daily into more absolute contempt'[51] . . . there were clear signs that the Government in London was determined to change everything in Scotland to an English model. This disturbed Scott very deeply, and as we shall see, this was one of the strongest emotional forces in his life.

With the important exception of this key issue (which I shall consider in a later chapter), Scott achieved a conscious and satisfying balance between the diverse impulses of his mind. The way in which he could criticise and mock the 'nonsensical trash' of his romantic reading, the 'romantic idealisation of Scottish aristocracy', his 'Gothic' tastes, the 'regiment of horse' exercising in his head and so forth, shows, I think, that he was at peace with them, understood them for what they were, and had reduced them to a proper proportion in his thoughts. The overwhelming impression which he made on his contemporaries who knew him, and on his readers ever since, is one of sanity, balance and fair-mindedness. In his *Memories of Sir Walter Scott* Skene constantly uses such phrases as 'his habitual kind and gentle temper', 'his habitual good humour'.[52] 'Somehow or other,' Washington Irving wrote to him, 'there is a genial sunshine about you that warms every creeping thing into heart and confidence'.[53]

The conflicts in Scott's mind, if that is what they were, were not destructive. They were diverse facets of a complex personality who was receptive to a vast range of impulses from Ariosto to Adam Smith, but who accorded them all their due place. They were all part of his strength as a novelist because they meant that he understood, and sympathised with, a wide range of human character and human behaviour. This wide tolerance accounts too, I think, for his fair-mindedness. 'Part of their astonishing freshness, their perennial vitality' Virginia Woolf wrote of the Waverley novels, 'is that you may read them over and over again, and never know for certain what Scott himself was or what Scott himself thought.'[54] There is a sense in which this is true. You would never guess from *Old Mortality*, if that was all you had to go on, that Scott admired Claverhouse and disliked the Covenanters; he is fair and frank about the vices and virtues of both sides. But you would know, I think, that he was on the side of Morton, the man in the middle, and against the excesses both of fanatical devotion and arbitrary power. Even there, his honesty compels him to show that in the circumstances of the time, moderation was bound to be ineffective.

At the same time, as many people have remarked, there is an air of melancholy and pessimism about much of his work, which is strange for a man apparently so serene, convivial and at peace with the world. Robert Gordon finds that *The Bride of Lammermoor* 'is really a lamentation over the death of ancient Scottish strength and virtue in a world governed by rich money-snobs with connexions in the corrupt and dominant city of London'.[55] Thomas Crawford speaks of the strain of melancholy which runs through so much of Scott's prose and verse as 'mourning for Scotland's vanished independence',[56] and he quotes[57] from *The Lay of the Last Minstrel* (it is from the invocation to Scotland 'O Caledonia! Stern and wild', in the introduction to Canto 6th):

> Still as I view each well-known scene,
> Think what is now, and what hath been,
> Seems as, to me, of all bereft,
> Sole friends they woods and streams were left;
> And thus I love them better still,
> Even in extremity of ill.

The explanation for this melancholy, the conspicuous exception to his genial tolerance, is to be found in his feelings about the historical fate of Scotland. In December 1827 when he was discussing in the *Journal* the arrangement of the volumes of his *Tales of a Grandfather*, he wrote this:

> . . . for surely we ought to close one volume at least of Scottish history at a point which leaves the kingdom triumphant and happy; and, alas! where do her annals present us with such an era excepting after Bannockburn?[58]

I think that this air of melancholy and pessimism and the reasons for it are one of the essential clues to an understanding of Scott and of his attitude to Scotland.

NOTES

Chapter quotation: G. Gregory Smith, *Scottish Literature: Character and Influence,* p. 4 (London, 1919).
[1] op cit, p. 4.
[2] **Irving, Washington,** *Abbotsford and Newstead Abbey,* p. 45 (London, 1850).
[3] **Scott, P. H.,** 'Severitas: The Romano-Scottish Ideal', *Blackwood's Magazine,* pp. 414–419 (November 1976).

4 **Scott, Sir Walter,** *Journal,* p. 112. Ed. D. Douglas (Edinburgh, 1891).

5 **Lockhart, J. G.,** *Life,* Vol. II, Chapter XX, p. 130 (1837-38).

6 ibid, Vol. III, Chapter XXXV, pp. 26-27.

7 ibid, Vol. I, Chapter I, p. 35.

8 ibid, Vol. I, Chapter I, p. 35.

9 **Muir, Edwin,** *Scott and Scotland,* p. 144 (London, 1936).

10 **Scott, Sir Walter,** *Familiar Letters,* Vol. I, p. 28. Ed. D. Douglas (Edinburgh, 1894).

11 *Journal,* p. 526.

12 **Ford, Boris,** *The Pelican Guide to English Literature, Vol. 5: From Blake to Byron,* p. 111 (Harmondsworth, 1977).

13 *Bicentenary Essays,* pp. 26-27.

14 **Brown, David,** *Walter Scott and the Historical Imagination,* p. 94 (London, 1979).

15 **Scott, Sir Walter,** *The Lives of the Novelists,* pp. 196-7 (Everyman's Library edition, 1928).

16 ibid, pp. 198-99.

17 Waverley Novels, *Magnus Opus* edition (reprint of 1895), Vol. 15, p. 14.

18 ibid, Vol. 2, p. 418.

19 ibid, Vol. 15, p. 289.

20 ibid, Vol. 15, p. 295.

21 ibid, Vol. 15, p. 303.

22 **Lockhart, J. G.,** *Life,* Vol. V, Chapter LXXXIV, p. 439.

23 ibid, Vol. IV, Chapter LXIV, pp. 329-30.

24 **Hogg, James,** *Familiar Anecdotes of Sir Walter Scott,* Ed. by D. S. Mack, p. 95 (Edinburgh, 1972).

25 **Scott, Sir Walter,** *The Tales of a Grandfather,* p. 751 (Edinburgh edition of 1889).

26 **Lockhart, J. G.,** *Life,* Vol. 1, Chapter I, pp. 29-47.

27 ibid, Vol. IV, Chapter LXIV, p. 329.

28 *Journal,* p. 550.

29 **Lockhart, J. G.,** *Life,* Vol. IV, Chapter LXIII, pp. 294-5.

30 op cit, p. 13.

31 **Smith, Sydney,** *Letters,* Ed. by N. C. Smith, Letter of 28th December 1823 to Archibald Constable, Vol. I, p. 405 (Oxford, 1953).

32 Waverley Novels, Vol. 14, pp. 398 and 399.

33 ibid, Vol. 14, p. 374.

34 ibid, Vol. 14, p. 374.

34 ibid, Vol. 5, p. 33.

35 **Scott, Sir Walter,** *Lives of the Novelists,* pp. 191-2 (Everyman's Library edition 1928).

36 This phrase can possibly be ascribed to Virginia Woolf.

[37] **Scott, Sir Walter,** *Familiar Letters,* Ed. D. Douglas (Edinburgh, 1894), Vol. 1, p. 215.

[38] Introduction to *Lay of Last Minstrel,* O.S.A., p. 50.

[39] **Lockhart, J. G.,** *Life,* Vol. I, Chapter XIV, p. 415.

[40] ibid, Vol. I, Chapter I, p. 37.

[41] Waverley Novels, Vol. 35, p. 68.

[42] **Scott, Sir Walter,** *Letters of Malachi Malagrowther, Miscellaneous Prose,* Vol. 1, p. 747 (edition of 1847).

[43] **Sir Walter Scott,** *Letters,* Ed. by H. Grierson (1932-37), Vol. 9, p. 437.

[44] **Scott,** *Letters of Malachi Malagrowther* (as 42 above), p. 727.

[45] *Familiar Letters,* Vol. 1, pp. 66-7.

[46] *Letters,* Vol. 3, p. 302.

[47] **Lockhart, J. G.,** *Life,* Vol. V, Chapter LXXVI, p. 211.

[48] **Scott, Sir Walter,** Review of Cromek's *Reliques of Robert Burns.* Quoted by A. M. Clark in *Sir Walter Scott: The Formative Years,* p. 78 (Edinburgh, 1969).

[49] Waverley Novels, Vol. 36, p. 369.

[50] As, for example, in **Donald Carswell,** *Sir Walter: A Four-Part Study in Biography,* p. 161 (London, 1930).

[51] **Scott, Sir Walter,** *Letters of Malachi Malagrowther* (as note 42), p. 725.

[52] op cit, pp. 189 and 124 (London, 1909).

[53] *Familiar Letters,* Vol. 2, p. 60.

[54] **Woolf, Virginia,** 'The Antiquary' in *Collected Essays,* Vol. 1, p. 141 (London, 1966).

[55] **Gordon, Robert C.,** *Under Which King? A Study of the Scottish Waverley Novels,* p. 106 (1969).

[56] **Crawford, Thomas,** *Scott,* p. 43 (Edinburgh and London, 1965).

[57] ibid, p. 39.

[58] *Journal,* p. 511.

3

Sandy-Knowe

'He was makin' himsel' *a' the time'*

The fragment of autobiography[1] which Scott wrote at Ashesteil in 1808 covers only about forty pages of print. It breaks off, apparently in mid-paragraph, at the point when he had just passed his trials as an advocate in July 1792, a month or so before his twenty-first birthday. Short as it is, it reveals, like a case study in the importance of early experiences, the roots of the 'combination of opposites' in Scott's mind and feelings. There are many other passages of autobiography scattered through his works, especially in the Introduction to the narrative poems and in those which he wrote between 1829 and 1832 for the *magnum opus* collected edition of the novels. The opening of *Redgauntlet* is a thinly disguised autobiography in itself. Most of these refer to the same early period, and only confirm and elaborate the admirably succinct account of 1808. Even the *Journal* written in the years of struggle at the end of his life, from 1825 to 1832, show that the same impulses had not lost their force. If he was diverse, he was also consistent.

The events recorded in the Ashesteil paper are meagre enough. He was born in Edinburgh in 1771,[2] the son of a moderately prosperous, benevolent but austere Writer to the Signet. When he was eighteen months old he lost the power in his right leg, which left him lame for life. In search of a cure, he was sent to his grandfather's farm of Sandy-Knowe, in the Borders, beneath the ancient tower of Smailholm. There he spent about three years, apart from a visit to Bath. He returned to Edinburgh and went to the High School. He was again ill and spent another six months in the Borders, this time

26

at Kelso. Then Edinburgh University, apprenticeship in his father's law office, another serious illness and back to the University to prepare for the bar. In this he was successful – and that is where his account ends. Not, one might think, a very eventful or auspicious start to life. But what mattered was not the external events, but the impulses to his mind and imagination and they were rich and various. It began at Sandy-Knowe, of which Scott, although he was only between two and four years old at the time, had a very vivid memory. The place has changed little. Even today, it is impossible to visit the tower of Smailholm, a few steps away from the farm-house, without irresistibly feeling the atmosphere of the Border wars and forays. Scott was overwhelmingly susceptible to the atmosphere:

> And still I thought that shatter'd tower
> The mightiest work of human power;
> And marvell'd as the aged hind
> With some strange tale bewitch'd my mind,
> Of forayers, who with headlong force,
> Down from that strength had spurr'd their horse, . . .
> Of patriot battles, won of old
> By Wallace wight and Bruce the bold; . . .
> And onward still the Scottish Lion bore,
> And still the scatter'd Southron fled before.[3]

Scott might have said like Burns, 'the story of Wallace poured a Scottish prejudice in my veins which will boil along there till the flood-gates of life shut in eternal rest'.[4]

The Borderer has always been especially susceptible to these feelings because of the proximity of the 'auld enemy'. Edwin Muir, by the way, once made precisely this point in conversation with George Bruce to explain the reaction of people like Francis George Scott and Hugh MacDiarmid to his book *Scott and Scotland*. They were Borderers and the Borders 'had experienced the threat of destruction by the English over a long period of history'; Muir came from the northern islands and was remote from all that.[5]

In going to Sandy-Knowe, Scott was in a real sense going home. He described his father as a Borderer, for although an Edinburgh lawyer he was the first member of his family to move to the town and adopt a learned profession. On both his father's and his mother's

27

side, Scott was descended from Border families celebrated in history, legend and ballad, and not many generations back. His grandfather, Beardie, so called from his beard which he refused to cut until the Stuarts were restored, had been *out* in 1715. His grandfather, in turn, was Auld Watt of Harden, a hero of Border legend. The real name of both of these worthies was also Walter Scott. At Sandy-Knowe, their descendant was filled with tales of their exploits. His Jacobite feeling, Scott says, 'was deeply confirmed by the stories told in my hearing of the cruelties exercised in the executions at Carlisle, and in the Highlands, after the battle of Culloden. One or two of our own distant relations had fallen on that occasion, and I remember of detesting the name of Cumberland with more than infant hatred'.

But the older Border tradition was still more persuasive. 'The local information, which I conceive had some share in forming my future taste and pursuits, I derived from the old songs and tales which then formed the amusement of a retired county family. My grandmother in whose youth the old border depredations were matter of recent tradition, used to tell me many a tale of Watt of Harden, Wight Willie of Aikwood, Jamie Tellfer of the fair Dodhead, and other heroes.'[6]

Even before he could read, his aunt used to read books to him until he knew long passages by heart, something for which he had a remarkable facility almost to the end of his life. The ballad of 'Hardyknute' was one of the first. Scott was a captive, if willing and enthusiastic audience, because for a time he could not walk and the ballads and stories had to take the place of all the ordinary childhood pleasures. If the conspicuous part played by his own ancestors in their tales of Border exploits encouraged family pride, Sandy-Knowe was also, in the Scottish way, unpretentious and egalitarian. He spent his days with an old cow-bailie who was the 'aged hind' who told him the stories of Smailholm.

The Border traditions, in which Scott was thus immersed before he was six, were those of a frontier society which had taken the first brunt of the English attack in the war which lasted for a thousand years. They were accustomed to sudden alarms and attacks, to fire and the sword and to the loss of all they possessed. The countryside was strewn with the shattered ruins of abbeys and churches destroyed by the invader as recently as the reign of Henry VIII. This life had bred a sturdy, self-reliant people, with a clan system not unlike the Highlands, because mutual support of kinsman and neighbour was the best form of defence. If not exactly lawless, because it had its own rules and codes of behaviour, it was a society accustomed to take the law into its own hands. Even if the Borders were close to Edinburgh they remained for long inaccessible because of the bleak hills and lack of roads. Walter Scott himself was the first man to take a wheeled vehicle into Liddesdale. This inaccessibility meant that the writ of Edinburgh hardly ran there in the past, and when Border warfare ceased after 1603, it meant that traditions long remained in the memory. They were embodied in a rich oral literature, the Border ballads.

The ballads were not only one of the first literary influences on Scott, they must have had a particularly powerful effect because of the surroundings in which he first heard them and the associations with his own ancestors. It is not surprising, to anticipate a little, that Scott's first important book was his *Minstrelsy of the Scottish Border*, texts of ballads, collected, arranged and partly written by him over a period of nearly ten years. (He made his first 'raid' into Liddesdale in pursuit of texts in 1792, and the first two volumes of the book came out in 1802.) Like Burns with the songs, Scott had no hesitation in linking up scattered fragments and 'improving' imperfect lines. He had so absorbed the spirit of the ballads that it is now impossible to tell where tradition stops and Scott starts. 'Kinmont Willie' sounds both typical of the ballads and curiously Scott-like, and it is, in fact, possible that he wrote the whole of it himself. Some of the ballads are comic; some are about love, usually unhappy:

O waly, waly, but love be bony,
    A little time while it is new,
But when 'tis auld it waxeth cauld,
    And fades away like the Morning Dew[7]

Many are about the supernatural, stated quite naturally as part of life, but an uncanny and disturbing part:

It was mirk mirk night, and there was nae stern light,
    And they waded through red blude to the knee;
For a' the blude, that's shed on earth,
    Rins through the springs o' that countrie.[8]

As so often in *Waverley Novels*, there are omens, prophecies and dreams:

> But I hae dream'd a dreary dream,
>> Beyond the Isle of Skye;
> I saw a dead man win a fight,
>> And I think that man was I.[9]

Above all, the ballads are about raids, forays and battle. Scott liked to refer to them as 'Border – raid' ballads, and said that they were the sort of thing that his memory retained most tenaciously.[10] Edwin Muir suggests that this part of the ballad tradition accounts for the part which Scott assigns to fighting in his novels. 'His imagination was irresistibly attracted by interregnums of civilisation, by times when the normal conventions of civilised life were abrogated and it was not only a pleasure, but a permissible pleasure, for men to fight as much as they cared.'[11] I think that this is too narrow a view both of the ballads and of Scott. They are certainly ballads which seem to take pleasure in swashbuckling adventure without thought of the consequences, just as one side of Scott was attracted by romantic ideas of soldiering, particularly in the cavalry, which was the closest he could get in his day to the life of a Border reiver. But Scott, in the end was always on the side of stability and peace, and the ballads predominantly take a tragic view of war:

> But think no ye my heart was sair,
>> When I laid the moul' on his yellow hair;
> O think no ye my heart was wae,
>> When I turn'd about, away to gae?[12]

How could it be otherwise in a countryside that had so often been laid waste by invasion?

The relationship of the narrative poems, *The Lay of the Last Minstrel* and *Marmion* especially, to the ballads is obvious. The relationship with the novels is less apparent, even if 'Wandering Willie's Tale' is a ballad in prose and *The Bride of Lammermoor* another of greater length. Both the ballads and the novels embrace the supernatural. If in Scott it is inevitably more contrived and handled with apology and scepticism, the work of his contemporary Borderer, James Hogg, is a reminder that the supernatural tradition of the ballad was by no means dead. As for method in a more general sense, is there any connection between Scott's often long-winded prose and reluctance to come to the point and the directness and economy of the ballads, 'abrupt and laconic' as Henry Mackenzie called them?[13] They have in common a tendency to carry forward the action by means of dialogue, and Scott was perhaps influenced in this by the ballads. The best of Scott's dialogues were in the Scots language and so, of course, are the ballads. Edwin Muir in an earlier book, when he was in a less provocative mood, wrote: 'the ballads enshrine the very essence of the Scottish spirit, and they could have been written only in the Scottish tongue.'[14] The same might be said of the great conversations in the novels. Often, too, they make a point with an economy of words which is entirely in the ballad tradition:

'I dinna ken muckle about the law', answered Mrs Howden; 'but I ken, when we had a king, and a Chancellor, and parliament-men o' our ain, we could aye peeble them wi' stanes when they werena gude bairns – But naebody's nails can reach the length o' Lunnon.'[15]

Scott's raids in search of ballads had another important result; it brought him into touch with a great variety of people who were afterwards to reappear as characters in the novels. It was, after all, Dandie Dinmont country. He was looking not for written texts but for ballads still alive in the oral tradition. Not everybody approved. James Hogg's mother, one of his sources, said to him, 'there war never ane o' my sangs prentit till ye prentit them yoursel', an' ye hae spoilt them awthegether. They were made for singing an' no for reading; but ye hae broken the charm now, an' they'll never be sung mair. An' the worst thing of a', they're nouther right spell'd nor right setten down', and Hogg says that she was right in her prophecy.[16] Still, if Scott had not printed the texts, they might have been lost altogether, and that includes many of the finest. In the course of this search, wandering, as Lockhart says, from the shepherd's hut to the minister's manse, and exploring every peel from foundation to battlement, Scott became intimately familiar with the whole countryside and with everything and everybody in it. This was all stored away in his formidable memory as part of his comprehensive grasp of the Scottish reality. He was helped by the incomparable John Leyden[17] and often accompanied by Robert Shortreed, the Sheriff-Substitute of Roxburghshire. 'Sic an' endless fund o' humour and drollery as he then had wi' him', Shortreed recalled. 'Never ten yards but we were either laughing or roaring or singing. Wherever we stopped, how brawlie he suited himsel' to everybody! He aye did as the lave did; never made himsel' the great man, or took ony airs in the company. . . . He was makin' himsel' a' the time, but he didna ken maybe what he was about till years had passed: At first he thought o' little, I daresay, but the queerness and the fun.'[18]

Of course, the humour and the drollery, the conversations at Sandy-Knowe and all over the Borders were in Scots. Henry Cockburn, who was eight years younger than Scott, writing in his *Journal* in 1844, regretted the decline in the use of Scots during his own lifetime. But he adds, 'when I was a boy no Englishman could have addressed the Edinburgh populace without making them stare, and probably laugh. We looked upon an English boy at the High School as a ludicrous and incomprehensible monster'.[19] If this were so in Edinburgh, we may be sure that the Borders were even more strongly monolingual in Scots. I am sure that Kurt Wittig is right in saying that the rhythms and phrases of Scott's dialogue came more from living example than from literature.[20] In his raids through the Borders, Scott was collecting not only ballads and characters, but the anecdotes and phrases which enlivened his novels and his own conversation for the rest of his life.

That Scott's handling of the Scots language is the greatest of his literary achievements is beyond dispute. It has been noticed by English writers, even if the English are usually unreceptive to the Scots language. Lord David Cecil, for instance: 'Scott's vernacular dialogue is style in its highest sense; every image apt, every cadence exact to follow the modulation of the speaker's mood, yet never unmusical. He has achieved that rarest of literary triumphs, a form of speech which sounds perfectly natural and which is yet as expressive as poetry.'[21] Or the German, Kurt Wittig: 'The Scots style . . . the rich vivid idioms, the pregnant and suggestive simplicities, the apt and pithy force, the subtle humour, the bold comparisons, and above all the rhythm of Scots speech, . . . Scots thus assumes a semi-poetic quality by its undercurrent of rhythm and submerged music. The vernacular, to Scott, is the language of the heart, and his Scots passages are fraught with a higher significance and strike at the very core of feeling; and in moments of deepest feeling, the suggestive terseness of Scots enables him to be more sharply realistic and supremely articulate.' '. . . It is here, and in interspersed lyrics from the mouths of the same people that Scott rises to sublime heights . . . Scott usually is greatest when most Scottish.'[22] Virginia Woolf: 'the lifeless English turns to living Scots. . . . One is tempted, indeed, to suppose that he did it, half-consciously, on purpose – he showed up the language of the fine gentlemen who bored him by the immense vivacity of the common people whom he loved. Images, anecdotes, illustrations, drawn from sea, sky, and earth, race and bubble from their lips. They shoot every thought as it flies, and bring it trembling to the ground in metaphor. Sometimes it is a phrase – "at the back of a dyke, in a wreath o' snow, or in the wame o' wave"; sometimes a proverb – "he'll no can haud down his head to sneeze, for fear o' seeing his shoon"; always the dialogue is sharpened and pointed by the use of that Scottish dialect which is at once so homely and so pungent, so colloquial and so passionate, so shrewd and so melancholy into the bargain.'[23]

Of course, his Scots, as Muir says, 'was far better than his English'.[24] There is really nothing mysterious about this because it was after all his mother tongue, his first and natural language. It was spoken all around him at Sandy-Knowe, and in the streets of Edinburgh and indeed in the drawing rooms because even men like David Hume, who wrote impeccable English prose, always spoke Scots. Edward Topham, an English visitor to Edinburgh in 1774, said of the great *literati*, 'they appear to me, from their conversation, to write English as a foreign tongue; their mode of talking, phrase and expression, but little resembling the language of their works'.[25] Almost always when people write a foreign language they lose the flexibility, subtlety, wit and spirit which they might have in their own and grow ponderous and dull. They are afraid to shoot the thought as it flies because they might be making a linguistic mistake. If Scott's English prose is often no more than plain and competent, and at its worst, pompous and flat-footed, it was because he was denying himself the pith and pungency of his natural speech. It is pitiful to think how much has been lost, both in literature and in ordinary everyday communication, because of the slow and steady pressures against the use of Scots.

Perhaps it was more than a linguistic loss. In his book, *The Author of Waverley*, D. D. Devlin says: 'It is often remarked that

33

Scott's strength lies in the handling of the vernacular. What perhaps needs saying is that his strength lies here not simply because he had an ear for lowland speech, but because he endorsed those qualities of mind and character which the vernacular so accurately conveyed.'[26] This is essentially the same point as the one which Edwin Muir made about the ballads, that their spirit was so Scottish that they could not be expressed in any other tongue. If these remarks are true, as I think they are, it means that there is such an intimate relationship between language and personality, that if a language is eroded, then the personality expressed through it is eroded as well. We know, for example, from Henry Cockburn,[27] that the Scots language was in a period of marked decline during Scott's lifetime. His use of it therefore had more than simply literary significance. It was an act of national self-defence.

It is a measure of Scott's skill in writing dialogue that he managed to make the Scots convincing and at the same time intelligible, without too much difficulty, even to a reader with no previous knowledge of the language. Partly he achieves this by the device of having at least one of the speakers in each conversation speak English, even when this does violence to probability. If you could understand one side of the conversation, you could make a pretty good guess at the other. Take this conversation between Henry Morton and Cuddie Headrigg, for example:

> 'And what is your object, Cuddie? and how can I be of use to you?'
>
> 'Wark, stir, wark and a service, is my object – a bit beild for my mither and myself – we hae gude plenishing o' our ain, if we had the cast o' a cart to bring it down – and milk and meal, and greens enow, for I'm gleg at meal-time, and sae is my mither, lang may it be sae – And, for the pennyfee and a' that, I'll just leave it to the laird and you. I ken ye'll no see a poor lad wranged, if ye can help it.'
>
> Morton shook his head. 'For the meat and lodging, Cuddie, I think I can promise something; but the penny-fee will be a hard chapter, I doubt.'
>
> 'I'll take my chance o't, stir,' replied the candidate for service, 'rather than gang down about Hamilton, or any sic far country.'
>
> 'Well; step into the kitchen, Cuddie, and I'll do what I can for you.'[28]

Now, it is very unlikely that a laird's son at the end of the seventeenth century would ever have spoken prissy English of that kind. A sensible man, even if he had English, would not use it with

34

someone like Cuddie. This is deliberate distortion for the sake of intelligibility, and for the sake of an audience outside Scotland.

These questions of the ballads and the Scots language have taken us some distance away from Sandy-Knowe, but this serves to emphasise the extent to which most of the dominant influences on Scott were present before he was six; the poetry, the romance, the feeling for the supernatural, family pride and egalitarianism, the passion for Scotland. Some of these influences were strengthened indirectly from his illness, which took him to Sandy-Knowe in the first place. The long periods of inactivity made him more dependent on reading and the exercise of his imagination than he might have been otherwise. His illness meant, too, that he spent a lot of time with people of his grandfather's generation, whose stories and reminiscences could carry him back seventy or eighty years. Consciously or not, he had started to build up in his mind a picture of the Scottish past, particularly of the recent past, where the books and records could be given flesh and bones by living memory. Eventually he also acquired a complete knowledge of the written records and literature, having the luck to have a photographic or tape-recorder memory which could remember long texts after one reading or one hearing. This vast knowledge, ranging from obscure and ancient documents to the chance remark of someone who had taken part, was all within immediate recall. When he was at work on *Tales of a Grandfather*, he noted in the *Journal* on 11th October 1827 that he had written forty pages in one day, 'but then the theme was so familiar, being Scottish history, that my pen never rested.'[29] In April 1829, when his health was finally breaking down and he was hard pressed with other work, he debated with himself whether he should accept a commission to write a History of Scotland in one volume. He wrote in the *Journal*; 'This would be very easy work. I have the whole stuff in my head, and could write *currente calamo*',[30] and he did, within a few months.

While Scott was at Sandy-Knowe he was taken to Bath for a year in the hope that the waters might do some good for his lameness. Bath had at least two good results. He saw a performance of *As You Like It*, and was so introduced to Shakespeare, the first of the many enthusiasms and influences external to Scotland. About fifty years later, he wrote in his *Journal*: 'I have a particular respect for *As You Like It*. It was the first play I ever saw, and that was at Bath in 1776 or

35

1777. That is not yesterday, yet I remember the piece very well.'[31] Scott's writing is full not only of quotations from Shakespeare, but of allusions, hints, similarities and overtones. When Waverley 'could not but observe that in those towns in which they proclaimed James the Third, "no man cried God bless him!"',[32] he is quoting *Richard II*. It is not surprising that Ravenswood is reminded by the three hags met to prepare the body of Alice for burial of Macbeth's meeting with the three witches.[33] Perhaps it is in touches like these, apart from the wealth of character, that make so many people compare Scott with Shakespeare. It seems to me that the resemblances with Shakespeare are in surface ornament, not in anything essential; none of Scott's ideas or attitudes are derived from Shakespeare, although Shakespeare often gives him language to express what he wants to say. Gladstone compared *The Bride of Lammermoor* with *Romeo and Juliet*.[34] Certainly, there is a similarity in the basic situation but Scott took his plot from something which had actually happened in Scotland and the atmosphere and motivation are worlds apart. Scott sums up succinctly himself in his *Journal*, starting with a reference to Burns:

> Long life to thy fame and peace to thy soul, Rob Burns! When I want to express a sentiment which I feel strongly, I find the phrase in Shakespeare – or thee. The blockheads talk of my being like Shakespeare – not fit to tie his brogues.[35]

The other event at Bath was the time spent with John Home, a close friend of David Hume, the author of ('Whaur's your Willie Shakespeare noo?') *Douglas*, and one of the great figures of Enlightenment Edinburgh. He 'paid much attention', says Scott, 'to my aunt and me'.[36] That is all he says about it, but it is certain that with his strong intelligence, vigorous imagination and prodigious memory he would not have failed to respond to this first introduction to the other great influence on his life, the counterpoise to Sandy-Knowe, the Edinburgh of the Enlightenment.

NOTES

Chapter quotation: Robert Shortreed, quoted in Lockhart's *Life*, Vol. I, Chapter VII, p. 168.
[1] See Chapter 1, p. 4, Note 18.

[2] **Clark, Arthur Melville,** *Sir Walter Scott, The Formative Years,* Chapter 1 (Edinburgh and London, 1969). He argues, using evidence which I do not find entirely convincing, that Scott was born on 15th August 1770, not on the same date in 1771, as generally accepted.

[3] **Scott, Sir Walter,** *Marmion,* Introduction to Canto Third, O.S.A., pp. 114–115.

[4] **Burns, Robert,** *Letters,* Ed. by De Lancey Ferguson, Oxford, 1931; Letter of 2nd August 1787 to Dr John Moore; Vol. 1, p. 106.

[5] **Bruce, George,** 'The Borderer and the Arcadian' in *The Age of MacDiarmid,* Ed. by P. H. Scott and A. C. Davies (Edinburgh, 1980), p. 101.

[6] **Lockhart, J. G.,** *Life,* Vol. I, Chapter 1, p. 14.

[7] *Border Ballads,* Ed. by William Beattie (Penguin Poets, 1952), 'Waly, Waly, gin love be bonny', p. 227.

[8] ibid, 'Thomas the Rhymer', p. 225.

[9] ibid, 'The Battle of Otterbourne', p. 36.

[10] **Lockhart, J. G.,** *Life,* Vol. I, Chapter 1, p. 28.

[11] **Muir, Edwin,** *Scott and Scotland,* pp. 167–168.

[12] **Beattie,** op cit, 'The Lament of the Border Widow', p. 162.

[13] Quoted in H. W. Thompson, *A Scottish Man of Feeling,* p. 67 (Oxford, 1931).

[14] **Muir, Edwin,** *Latitudes,* p. 30 (London, 1924).

[15] Waverley Novels, Vol. 12, p. 57.

[16] **Hogg, James,** op cit (Note 24, Chapter 2, p. 14), p. 137.

[17] **Scott, P. H.,** 'John Leyden: Polymath and Border Reiver', *Blackwood's Magazine,* October and November 1978.

[18] **Lockhart, J. G.,** *Life,* Vol. 1, Chapter VII, pp. 168 and 170.

[19] **Cockburn, Henry,** *Journal,* Vol. II, p. 88 (Edinburgh, 1874).

[20] **Wittig, Kurt,** *The Scottish Tradition in Literature,* p. 236 (Edinburgh and London, 1958).

[21] **Cecil, Lord David,** *Sir Walter Scott,* p. 38 (London, 1933).

[22] **Wittig, Kurt,** op cit, pp. 230, 232, 235.

[23] **Woolf, Virginia,** op cit (Chapter 1, p. 2, Note 16), pp. 136 and 141.

[24] op cit, p. 174.

[25] **Topham, Edward,** *Letters from Edinburgh 1774-75,* p. 55 (London, 1776). Facsimile reprint, Edinburgh, 1971).

[26] op cit, p. 125 (London, 1971).

[27] op cit (19 above), Vol. I, p. 189, Vol. II, pp. 88–89.

[28] Waverley Novels, Vol. 10, pp. 108–109.

[29] *Journal,* p. 46.

[30] ibid, p. 682.

[31] *Journal,* p. 410.

[32] Waverley Novels, Vol. 2, p. 250.

[33] Waverley Novels, Vol. 14, p. 359.

[34] **Colvin, Sir Sydney,** *Memories and Notes of Persons and Places, 1852-1914,* p. 198 (London, 1921).
I am indebted to David Brown's *Walter Scott and the Historical Imagination* for this reference. See pp. 135 and 141.

[35] *Journal*, p. 321.

[36] **Lockhart, J. G.,** *Life*, Vol. I, Chapter 1, p. 17.

4

Edinburgh: The High School

'The usual round of other Edinburgh boys, the High School and the college'

Arthur Melville Clark says rather sadly in his book on Scott that it has to be recognised that Scott and his Edinburgh contemporaries were less devoted to the University than to the High School.[1] They had none of the affection and sense of belonging for the University which they had for the school. This is certainly true, but it is also strange because life at the High School at that period was harsh and demanding. It was not an experience which anyone enjoyed much at the time. 'Did I ever pass unhappy years anywhere?' Scott asked himself in his *Journal* on 4th April 1826, 'None that I remember, save those at the High School, which I thoroughly detested on account of the confinement,' although he adds, 'I disliked serving in my father's office, too, from the same hatred to restraint.' His account of the school in the Ashesteil *Memoir* only warms into affection when he speaks of the Rector, Dr Alexander Adam, 'to whom I owed so much – a man so learned, so admirably adapted for his station, so useful, so simple, so easily contented'. Adam's qualities are evident to this day in Raeburn's portrait of him which is radiant with benevolence. But Scott goes on to speak of a 'savage fellow, called Nicol, one of the undermasters' who insulted Adam and challenged his authority. 'This man was an excellent classical scholar, and an admirable convivial humorist (which latter quality recommended him to the friendship of Burns);

but worthless, drunken, and inhumanly cruel to the boys under his charge.'[2] This was, indeed, the Willie who 'brew'd a peck o' maut',[3] but who was plainly abominable as a schoolmaster. Years later Scott wrote about the School with greater warmth, especially in the first chapter of *Redgauntlet*, published in June 1824. In October of the same year, he spoke at the opening of the Edinburgh Academy. He was at pains to emphasise that the new foundation was not intended to damage the High School, the 'pride and boast of our city'.[4]

Henry Cockburn, who went to the High School eight years after Scott, was one of those who suffered under Nicol. 'Out of the whole four years of my attendance there were probably not ten days in which I was not flogged at least once.' He too admired Adam – 'born to teach Latin, some Greek and all virtue . . . inspiring . . . enthusiastically delighted with every appearance of talent or goodness . . . and constantly under the strongest sense of duty'. But, he adds, 'the hereditary evils of the system and of the place were too great for correction even by Adam; and the general tone of the school was vulgar and harsh. . . . Two of the masters, in particular, were so savage, that any master doing now what they did every hour, would certainly be transported'.[5] Scott did not think that it was as bad as all that. 'I was indifferently well beaten at school', he wrote in the *Journal* on 13th December 1826, 'but I am now certain that twice as much discipline would have been well bestowed.'

But there was clearly more to the High School than the harshness of some of the masters, which was common enough in schools everywhere for at least another hundred years. When Samuel Johnson came to Scotland in 1773, he was determined to find fault with everything and not least with the state of scholarship, the universities and the schools; but, says Boswell, 'I brought him to confess that the High School of Edinburgh did well'.[6] Boswell, although, exceptionally, he did not go to the school himself, took a close interest in it. On 16th September 1780, for example, 'Mr Fraser, one of the masters of the High School, drank tea with us and examined the young Campbells excellently well, to settle what classes they should attend'.[7] This was Luke Fraser, Scott's first master at the school, whom he calls 'a good Latin Scholar and a very worthy man'.[8] Then, on 19th September, Boswell was 'present at Mr Fraser's opening his class with a decent prayer, after which I heard him examine some of the boys on a passage of Caesar. I was

40

much pleased with his perfect investigation of the elements of Latin and with his instruction in the sense, particularly the geography'.[9] (Although neither Boswell not Scott mention meeting the other, Scott was a member of Luke Fraser's class from 1778 to 1782 and was presumably there on that day.) On 22nd September, Boswell was at a dinner party with Dr Adam: 'Found my association of ideas in my boyish days as to the High School dissolved. Saw it as a good place for education.'[10] Next year, on 21st February 1781, Boswell 'went to the play of *Henry IV, First Part*, and saw all the High School in the theatre. It was a fine scene of boyish amusement and tumult. The profits of the play went to pay for the new school. So all the masters and all the boys were there'. It all gives a very different impression of the school from Cockburn's account.

The school, 'the most important in Scotland, and intimately connected with the literature and progress of the Kingdom', was, Lord Brougham said in a speech in 1825, 'invaluable . . . because men of the highest and lowest rank of society sent their children to be educated together'.[12] Probably the pre-eminence of the school was due to its long monopoly in the capital of the country, but, whatever the reason, a list of the men educated there reads like a biographical dictionary of the country's achievements. (It is particularly strong in literature – a tradition which continues with poets from William Drummond of Hawthornden in the sixteenth century to Norman MacCaig and Robert Garioch in the twentieth.) The mixture of classes was both an expression and a reinforcement of the constant Scottish tendency towards egalitarianism. 'I used to sit between a youth of a ducal family and the son of a poor cobbler,'[13] wrote William Steven in his *History* of the School, and this was typical. Or at least it was typical until it was destroyed by the aping of English behaviour in the nineteenth century when wealthier people started to send their sons to English class-conscious and class–exclusive schools. This is one of the ways in which so much that was valuable in the Scottish tradition has been damaged by English intervention and example.

The traditions of the school, the egalitarianism, even the rigours and the size of the classes – for there were one hundred boys in each – all contributed to a strong feeling of community, the sense of belonging, that Melville Clark noticed. At the school itself, there was a lively spirit of academic competitiveness, with boys constantly changing in precedence according to their performance. This was taken so seriously that even Scott was driven to a trick to gain a place. By the time they left, the boys knew one another so well and had been through so much together that there was a bond between them for life. Often in Scottish life, among the literati of the eighteenth century for instance, or among the Edinburgh Reviewers or between Scott and his friends, there is an atmosphere of easy familiarity, mutual trust and friendship, a desire to help and co-operate. At least part of the reason is that so many of the people involved were at the High School together.

Scott had an especial need for a community of this kind because of the isolation of his childhood, when he was cut off from other children by his illness. Even the return to live with his own brothers in Edinburgh was a shock. How was this cosseted and lame child to cope with a school, 'robust and competitive', [14] as Matthew McDiarmid puts it? Initially, it seems, by making up in spirit by what he lacked in physical agility. He had a determination to overcome his lameness which enabled him for years to compete with anyone on foot or horseback. In the first chapter of *Redgauntlet*, there is a footnote about the escapades of the boys of the High School on the Castle rock, where Scott recalls that he was once one of those 'juvenile dreadnoughts'. But he had another resource, drawing advantage from the hours which his lameness had forced him to spend in dreaming, reading and talk. 'In the winter play hours, when hard exercise was impossible, my tales used to assemble an admiring audience round Lucky Brown's fireside, and happy was he that he could sit next to the inexhaustible narrator.'[15] He had already started, like a latter day minstrel, to use his imagination and the stores of his memory to entertain.

John Fleming, in his admirable book on Robert Adam, says of the High School of about this time (Robert Adam was there about a generation before Scott), that a boy emerged from it 'with a sound knowledge of Latin grammar and literature, especially Cicero, but of nothing else. For nothing but Latin was taught at the High School'.[16] The only difference by Scott's time was that a little Greek had been added to the Latin. This concentration on Latin was not as crazy as it sounded. In the first place, the sort of analysis of a complex Latin sentence which is necessary to extract its meaning is about as good an exercise in logical thought as anyone has been able to devise.

It encourages the habit of the search for the meaning and the thought behind the surface of the words. The next step, the translation of a Latin text into one's own language, is a good exercise in the manipulation of words. You cannot translate from one language into another without deciding what it is you are trying to say, and this is an excellent antidote to vague thought and imprecise speech. On the other hand, the sentence structure of Latin is infectious with its tendency to run into an elaborate construction of dependent clauses. It is the style that Scott falls into when he is writing at speed, an echo of the years construing Cicero on the benches of the High School. And, of course, Scott continued to read Latin for pleasure and information for the rest of his life, even if he read more mediaeval chronicles than classical writers and his favourite Latin poet was the sixteenth-century Scot, George Buchanan.

Latin, however, was more than a linguistic exercise. Boswell talks about 'instruction in the sense, particularly the geography'. Both Scott and Cockburn say that Adam ran into trouble at the time of the French Revolution because he seemed to be supporting revolutionary principles when he talked about ancient Rome. 'He was no politician; insomuch that it may be doubted whether he ever knew one public measure or man from another. But a Latin and Greek schoolmaster naturally speaks about such things as liberty, and the people, and the expulsion of the Tarquins, and republics, and this was quite sufficient for the times; especially as any modern notions that he had were popular, and he was too honest, and too simple, to disguise them.'[17] Adam's book, *Roman Antiquities* was reprinted many times and is described by Melville Clark as 'still useful'.[18] In addition to a book on Latin and English grammar and a Latin dictionary, he also wrote about classical biography. His interest in Latin studies was not confined to the language and literature but included history, geography and politics, and his teaching did the same.

If Latin literature was so used to illustrate a whole society, it was also used to encourage certain ideals and standards of behaviour. Cockburn, in his famous phrase about Dr Adam, quite naturally mentioned 'all virtue' in the same breath as Latin and some Greek. This association between the morality of Presbyterian Scotland and of Republican Rome may seem paradoxical but the resemblance between the two moral codes is very close. R. H. Barrow in his

43

book, *The Romans*, has a list of the qualities which Romans admired and liked to think that they possessed: *pietas, gravitas* ('a sense of the importance of the matters in hand'), *constantia, firmitas, disciplina, industria* ('hard work'), *virtus* ('manliness or energy') and *frugalitas* ('simple tastes'). 'It might all be summed up,' Barrow says, 'in *severitas*, which means being stern with oneself.'[19] Add to these a respect for learning and you have a catalogue of the Scottish virtues. Boswell was always preaching these qualities to himself in his *Journals*: 'Remember everything may be endured . . . have constant command of yourself. . . . Be firm, and persist. . . . Never indulge your appetite without restraint.'[20] So was Scott, although with more of the restraint in practice to which Boswell only aspired. '*Agere atque pati Romanum est*',[21] as he said in his *Journal*, and he clearly used the word 'Roman' as a term of the highest praise. 'A Roman,' says Scott talking of Davie Deans in *The Heart of Midlothian*, 'would have devoted his daughter to death from different failings and motives, but not upon a more heroic principle of duty.'[22] It is the same sort of comparison which Stevenson causes Glenalmond to make of Hermiston: 'He has all the Roman virtues: Cato and Brutus were such.'[23]

In his *Scott and Scotland*, Edwin Muir says that he will be content if he can show 'that the discipline of Scots law was not an adequate complement to Scott's riotous imagination and violent feelings, that something else was required, and that the Scotland of his time could not supply it'.[24] Like so many of Muir's statements, part of this asserts something which can neither be proved nor disproved, and another part disregards the facts. The effect of Scots Law on Scott's imagination was important, as we can see from the novels, as a stimulus as well as a complement. I do not know how it is possible to decide whether or not it was adequate as a complement. But it was far from being the only one which the Scotland of Scott's time supplied. The first in time and quite possibly in importance, was the Romano-Scottish influence of the High School, which might almost have been designed to curb the excesses of unbridled imagination.

There is something strange in basing a whole system of education on a language and civilisation which flourished more than a thousand years earlier. Scott himself thought so. In his speech at the opening of the Edinburgh Academy, he spoke of the advantages of adding such things as mathematics, and one's own language, literature and history. 'He would have the youths taught to venerate the patriots and heroes of our own country, almong with those of Greece and Rome; to know the histories of Wallace and Bruce, as well as those of Themistocles and of Caesar; and that the recollection of the fields of Flodden and Bannockburn should not be lost in those of Platea and Marathon.'[25] No one, I suppose, would now defend the exclusive pre-occupation with ancient Rome. Even so the old High School system must have had some virtue, if we can judge by the qualities of mind and character in the men it produced.

NOTES

Chapter quotation: R. L. Stevenson, *Weir of Hermiston*, Chapter 2.
[1] **Clark, Arthur Melville,** *Sir Walter Scott: The Formative Years,* p. 287 (Edinburgh and London, 1969).
[2] **Lockhart, J. G.,** *Life,* Vol. I, Chapter 1, p. 25.
[3] **Burns, Robert,** 'Willie brew'd a peck o' maut', O.S.A. edition (1969), p. 378.
[4] **Lockhart, J. G.,** *Life,* Vol. IV, Chapter LX, p. 182.
[5] **Cockburn, Henry,** *Memorials of His Time* (1872 edition), pp. 3, 4 and 9.
[6] **Boswell, James,** *Journal of a Tour of the Hebrides with Samuel Johnson, L.L.D.,* O.S.A. edition (1934), p. 209.
[7] *Boswell: Laird of Auckinleck, 1778-1782,* Ed. by J. W. Reed and F. A. Pottle, p. 249 (New York, 1977).
[8] **Lockhart, J. G.,** *Life,* Vol. I, Chapter 1, p. 21.
[9] As Note 7, p. 250.
[10] ibid, p. 252.
[11] ibid, p. 285.
[12] Quoted in James Grant's *Old and New Edinburgh,* Vol. 1, pp. 110 and 114 (Edinburgh, 1880).
[13] **Steven, William,** *The History of the High School of Edinburgh,* pp. 191-2 (1849).
[14] *The Poems of Robert Fergusson,* Ed. by Matthew P. McDiarmid (S.T.S. edition, 1954), Introduction, p. 12.
[15] **Lockhart, J. G.,** *Life,* Vol. I, Chapter 1, p. 23.
[16] **Fleming, John,** *Robert Adam and his Circle in Edinburgh and Rome,* p. 77 (London, 1962).
[17] **Cockburn, Henry,** op cit, p. 5.
[18] op cit, p. 20.

[19] **Barrow, R. H.,** *The Romans* (Penguin Books, 1949; reprint of 1962), pp. 22-23. This paragraph summarises the argument of my essay, 'Severitas: The Romano-Scottish Ideal', in *Blackwood's Magazine* (November, 1976), pp. 414-419.

[20] *Boswell in Holland 1763-1764* (1952), Ed. by F. A. Pottle, pp. 376-378.

[21] *Journal,* p. 214 (22nd June 1826).

[22] Waverley Novels, Vol. 12, p. 344.

[23] **Stevenson, R. L.,** *Weir of Hermiston* (Nelson's Classics, edition N.D.), Chapter 2, p. 47.

[24] **Muir, Edwin,** op cit, p. 133.

[25] **Lockhart, J. G.,** *Life,* Vol. IV, Chapter LX, p. 184.

5

Edinburgh: The University and the Law

'I was, in short, like an ignorant gamester, who kept a good hand until he knew how to play it.'

'I left the High School,' says Scott in the Ashesteil *Memoir*, 'with a great quantity of general information, ill arranged, indeed, and collected without system, yet deeply impressed upon my mind; readily assorted by my power of connexion and memory, and gilded, if I may be permitted to say so, by a vivid and active imagination.'[1] He is talking, as the context makes perfectly clear, not of the classical studies of the school, but of his own private reading – 'ample and indiscriminating as it was indefatigable' – in history, poetry and romance.

While he was still at school, Scott also had a tutor at home, James Mitchell, who would certainly have disapproved of the poetical and romantic part of this reading, for he was on the extreme wing of the Kirk. From him, Scott learned writing, arithmetic and French, but also some divinity and church history. They argued together over the religious disputes in the Scotland of the seventeenth century, with Scott laying the foundations of his deep understanding of these matters which he shows in the novels. Scott's father, who indulged in church history in secret, would have agreed with James Mitchell, and disapproved of all the romantic side of Scott's reading. This was something which Scott pursued on his own account, secretly and probably with some sense of guilt, that it was time stolen from his serious studies. This is presumably what he means in the remarks, of

47

a kind which he made more than once, about being 'half-educated, almost wholly neglected and left to myself, stuffing my head with most nonsensical trash'.[2] He had access to a vast range of books in the magnificent circulating library, run by James Sibbald and founded by Allan Ramsay (where Scott first saw Robert Burns). 'I was plunged into this great ocean of reading without compass or pilot,' as he says in the general Preface to the Waverley Novels.[3] Twice his illnesses encouraged this, once when he was sent to Kelso for six months just after he left the High School and again, a couple of years later, when a serious haemorrhage kept him in bed for several weeks: 'unless when someone had the charity to play chess with me, I was allowed to do nothing save read, from morning to night'.[4]

At Kelso, Scott discovered two books which gave him particular pleasure. The first was Percy's *Reliques of Ancient Poetry*, which confirmed and justified the enthusiasm for the ballads, first awakened at Sandy-Knowe. 'As I had been from infancy devoted to legendary lore of this nature, and only reluctantly withdrew my attention, from the scarcity of materials and the rudeness of those which I possessed, it may be imagined but cannot be described, with what delight I saw pieces of the same kind which had amused my childhood, and still continued in secret the Delilahs of my imagination, considered as the subject of sober research, grave commentary, and apt illustration. . . . Nor do I believe I ever read a book half so frequently, or with half the enthusiasm.'[5]

The other discovery was Tasso and Ariosto in the translations of Hoole, which opened up for him the pleasures of Italian romantic poetry. He once infuriated the Greek class at the University by arguing in an essay that Ariosto was superior to Homer. So that he could read Italian poetry in the original, he spent part of the first money he earned on Italian lessons. For a period of his life, he read Boiardo and Ariosto every year. This phase of his reading was (he tells us in the General Preface to the Waverley Novels)[6] similar to that described for Edward Waverley in the second chapter of the novel, when he 'drove through the sea of books, like a vessel without a pilot or a rudder'.[7] Apart from the classics and the Italian poets, it included Shakespeare, Spenser and Milton, French romances and chronicles like those of Froissart and Brantôme, Spanish romances and the Icelandic sagas. Scott does not tell how and when he learned Spanish, although, with his High School Latin, ability to read it would come easily enough. He seems to have taught himself to read both Gaelic and Norse.[8] Attracted by what he had heard of German romanticism, and by the resemblance of the language to lowland Scots, he took lessons in German and his first published work were translations from Burger and Goethe.

As we have seen, Scott often affected to despise and regret the romantic part of his reading. 'I since have had too frequently reason to repent that few ever read so much, and to so little purpose. . . . I have read as much nonsense of this class as any man now living.'[9] The whole point of describing Edward Waverley's reading is to show how it misled him by giving him a false view of life, which is only gradually corrected as experience shows that things are not as his imagination, fed by these books, had made him suppose. On the other hand, Scott also admits that this sort of reading had crucial effects on his own literary development. He says in the general Preface that 'the success of a few ballads (meaning the translations from the German) had the effect of changing all the purpose and tenor of my life, and converting a painstaking lawyer of some years standing into a follower of literature.'[10] He said that it was the example of Cervantes that first gave him the idea of writing a novel,[11] and that his digressive technique was derived from Ariosto.[12] The novels are full of references to Cervantes and to the French chroniclers, Shakespeare and Spenser, but even more to Tasso and Ariosto and to almost all aspects of Italian art and life. As R. D. S. Jack has suggested, all this has the effect of placing Scotland in Scott's work firmly in its European context, similarly to the way in which the eighteenth-century Scottish philosophers thought in European terms. But Scotland remains at the centre. Scott's knowledge of Scotland was derived from every possible kind of personal contact and involvement; his knowledge of other countries came from books alone.

Part of his familiarity with Scottish life came from his habit of constant wandering which took him into almost every corner of the country. 'The love of natural beauty,' he says in the *Memoir*, 'more especially when combined with ancient ruins, or remains of our fathers' piety or splendour, became with me an insatiable passion, which, if circumstances had permitted, I would willingly have gratified by travelling over half the globe.'[14] Circumstances did not permit, and Scott's travelling was nearly all confined to Scotland. He went once to Dublin, several times to London, twice to Paris and once to Naples when he was close to death; but his childhood visit to Bath was the longest time he ever spent outside Scotland. From his schooldays, he defied his lameness by covering long distances on foot or horseback whenever he had the chance; it was, he said, by far his favourite amusement.[15] 'I greatly doubt, Sir', his father told him, 'you were born for nae better than a *gangrel scrape gut*.'[16] To the familiarity with the Borders which he began at Sandy-Knowe, Scott before long added the Highlands on legal business. There was one memorable occasion when he went into the country of *The Lady of the Lake* at the head of an escort of a sergeant and six men. All the time, he was adding to his repertoire of character and anecdotes, to his understanding of men and events, and to his view of recent history as seen through the eyes of people who were alive and involved at the time.

So the diverse influences on Scott went forward simultaneously, the oral tradition of the ballads and the Latin of the High School; the Italian romantic poets and philosophy of the University; the legendary history of the old chronicles and the realistic reminiscences of the eye witnesses. The two parts of Edinburgh symbolised the division. 'Yet in a real sense these works,' writes Alexander Welsh of the Waverley Novels, 'originate from the city of Edinburgh, and could not have been written by a citizen of any other land but Scotland. To the present day, from the window of a library or from the confusion of city traffic in Edinburgh, one can be shocked by the sudden prospect of sublime nature crowding in upon civilisation.'[17] In Scott's day, the contrast was still more blatant. The Old Town on the ridge of the High Street, had changed little since the Middle Ages, crowded, turbulent, warm-hearted, egalitarian and insalubrious. It was still as Scott described the Edinburgh of James IV:

> Pil'd deep and mossy, close and high,
> Mine own romantic town![18]

But in Scott's own life-time, the other Edinburgh, the New Town, was spreading its geometric patterns, 'the Heavenly City' of the Edinburgh Philosophers – 'ordered, elegant, rational, optimistic'.[19] Scott was born in the Old Town in a house afterwards demolished to make way for Robert Adam's University. Before he was four, his family had moved to George Square, one of the newest and the finest of Edinburgh Georgian squares. (Or it was the finest until the University of this century destroyed three-quarters of it, leaving the Scott house in a sad remnant of its original setting.) In every sense, Scott belonged both to old and new Edinburgh, the romantic and the philosophical.

Scott was at Edinburgh University for two different periods, from 1783 to 1786, and from 1789 to 1792, with three years' apprenticeship in his father's legal office in the interval. From the beginning it was clear that his father firmly intended, like Saunders Fairford in *Redgauntlet*, to see his son well and truly launched on a career in the law, but young Walter went along happily with the idea. The only question was not whether it should be the law, but which branch of the law, partnership with his father as a 'writer' or 'the more ambitious profession of the bar'.[20] The decision was left to the son, and, once it was taken, he threw himself into the studies for it, 'with stern, steady, and undeviating industry'.[21] For the whole of his working life, Scott was a practising Scots lawyer, as apprentice, advocate, Sheriff of Selkirk and as one of the Clerks to the Court of Session. Scott had his moments of disgust with his profession (and who does not?), but it was an essential part of his being. If *The Heart of Midlothian* is the only one of the novels which turns on a point of law, legal considerations, legal characters and legal language appear frequently in the others. Adolphus in his enquiry into the identity of the 'Author of Waverley', had no doubt that he must be a Scots lawyer, whatever else he was.

Edinburgh had lost the King and the Court in 1603 and Parliament and Government in 1707. It had therefore lost most of the attributes of a capital and with them Scotland had lost both the power to control her own affairs and to offer the scope which follows from that to men of talent and ambition. 'Thus London licks the butter off our bread, by opening a better market for ambition,' wrote Scott in his *Journal* on 24th March 1829, 'Were it not for the difference of the religion and laws, poor Scotland could hardly keep a man that is worth having'.[22] The arrangements made in 1707 guaranteed, in the terms of the Treaty itself, the continuation of the Scottish courts and legal system. A separate Act guaranteed the Church of Scotland and (Scott might have added) the four

Universities. Scotland as an entity survived mainly by virtue of these three institutions, the law, the Kirk and the educational system. Of the three the law was the most ancient and deeply rooted in the Scottish past, enacting a body of law and practice which had evolved over the centuries. The lawyers therefore felt themselves to be in a very particular sense the chief upholders of Scottish identity and tradition. 'It is not to be denied,' Lockhart wrote, 'that the Scottish lawyers have done more than any other class of their fellow-citizens, to keep alive the sorely threatened spirit of national independence.'[23] As Lord Cameron has pointed out, even the book which first gave 'philosophical cohesion and rational formulation' to Scots law, Lord Stair's *Institutions* of 1681, is redolent with the spirit of patriotism or, if you prefer, nationalism.[24] William Beattie quotes the English historian, Richard Pares:

> If you take your stand on the hill which leads from the New Town of Edinburgh to the Old about 10 o'clock in the morning, you will see gentlemen ascending it in the black clothes and the prosperous-looking hats which lawyers wear: these are the judges and the Faculty of Advocates who are going up the hill to administer the law of Scotland. They and their predecessors have played an important part as bearers and defenders of nationality. It is not for nothing that the great Sir Walter Scott was something in the law line.[25]

There was yet another reason why the Scots Bar was congenial to Scott; it had a great literary tradition, for, in the absence of other outlets for ambition, the law attracted many of the liveliest minds. According to Henry Cockburn, the habit of six months vacation in the year played a part as well:

> It is this abstraction from legal business that has given Scotland the greater part of literature that has adorned her. The lawyers have been the most intellectual class in the country. The society of the Outer House has given them every possible incitement, and the Advocates' Library has furnished them with the means and the temptation to read.[26]

This library, which has now become the National Library, has long been the greatest in the country. No less than David Hume was the Keeper from 1752 and 1757 and he was succeeded by Adam Ferguson. It would be no exaggeration to say that most of the great works of the Scottish Enlightenment, based as they were on wide reading in philosophy and history, would have been inconceivable without the resources of the Advocates' Library. In the generation before Scott, David Hume was trained in the law, Hailes, Kames and Monboddo were all judges, and James Boswell was a practising advocate. Among Scott's contemporaries, Cockburn became a judge and Jeffrey was not only the great editor of the *Edinburgh Review*, but for a time, Lord Advocate. In no other period and in no other country, have the law and literature been so closely allied. Scott gave us the feel of this with Pleydell in *Guy Mannering*, one of the most sympathetic of his legal characters. He is found 'surrounded with books, the best editions of the best authors, and in particular, an admirable collection of classics'. 'These,' said Playdell, 'are my tools of trade. A lawyer without history or literature is a mechanic, a mere working mason; if he possesses some knowledge of these, he may venture to call himself an architect'. And when Pleydell gave Mannering some notes of introduction, 'they were addressed to some of the first literary characters of Scotland – 'to David Hume, Esq.', 'To John Home, Esq.', 'To Dr Ferguson', 'To Dr Black', 'To Lord Kames', 'To Mr Hutton', 'To John Clerk, Esq. of Eldin', 'To Adam Smith Esq.', 'To Dr Robertson'. And, Scott adds, it was 'a circle never closed against strangers of sense and information, and which has perhaps at no period been equalled, considering the depth and variety of talent which it embraced and concentrated'.[27]

At the same period too, if not to some extent still, the lawyers unquestionably set the tone of Edinburgh life; they were both an intellectual and social *élite*. 'The Bar,' Lockhart wrote in 1819, 'is the great focus from which the rays of interest and animation are diffused throughout the whole mass of society, in this northern capital.'[28] He attributed this both to the laywers' defence of the 'spirit of national independence' and to their intellectual accomplishments. The regard in which advocates stood is obvious from the accounts of Scott's early journeys; he was received everywhere with respect simply because he was an advocate. In Edinburgh, legal influence was felt even in the style of conversation. 'The best table-talk of Edinburgh,' Lockhart says, 'was, and probably still is, in a very large measure made of brilliant disquisition – such as might be transferred without alteration to a professor's note-book, or the pages of a critical Review – and of sharp word-catchings, ingenious thrusting and parrying of dialectics, and all the quips and quibblets of bar pleading. It was the talk of society to which lawyers and lecturers had, for at least a hundred years, given the tone'.[29] More than a hundred years later, the American, H. W. Thompson, with some pardonable exaggeration, could still write:

> It must be a source of satisfaction to the legal profession throughout the world that the modern city most renowned for intellect was and is a lawyers' town.

Scott's professors at the University included several men of distinction. There was Dugald Stewart, for instance, whose 'eloquence', Scott says, 'riveted the attention even of the most volatile student',[31] but who is described by others, such as Cockburn, in much more lyrical terms:

> To me his lectures were like the opening of the heavens. I felt I had a soul. His noble views, unfolded in glorious sentences, elevated me into a higher world.[32]

In John Bruce's class, Scott was chosen to read an essay before Principal Robertson, one of the leaders of the Edinburgh Enlightenment and one of the most celebrated historians of his day. But it seems from Scott's own account that the lectures which impressed him most profoundly were those on Scots law by David Hume, the nephew of the philosopher and afterwards one of Scott's colleagues as a Clerk to the Court of Session. It is worth quoting the whole of the passage in which Scott describes them. It explains not only something of the appeal of Scots law to a man of Scott's tastes and disposition but also more than a little of the genesis of the Waverley Novels:

> I can never sufficiently admire the penetration and clearness of conception which were necessary to the arrangement of the fabric of law, formed originally under the strictest influence of feudal principles, and innovated, altered, and broken in upon by the change of times, of habits, and of manners, until it resembles some ancient castle, partly entire, partly ruinous, partly dilapidated, patched and altered during the succession of ages by a thousand additions and combinations, yet still exhibiting, with the marks of its antiquity, symptoms of the skill and wisdom of its founders, and capable of being analysed and made the subject of a methodical plan by an architect who can understand the

54

various style of the different ages in which it was subjected to alteration. Such an architect has Mr Hume been to the law of Scotland, neither wandering into fanciful and obstruse disquisitions, which are more the proper subject of the antiquary, nor satisfied with presenting to his pupils a dry and undigested detail of the laws in their present state, but combining the past state of our legal enactments with the present, and tracing clearly and judiciously the changes which took place, and the causes which led to them.[33]

Notice the word, 'architect', with its echo of the literary and historical studies of Pleydell. 'Capable of being analysed and made the subject of a methodical plan by an architect who can understand the various styles of the different ages' is a metaphorical statement of the 'philosophical' attitude to history of the Enlightenment. Earlier in his *Memoir*, Scott had described the state of his historical studies when he left the High School:

The philosophy of history, a much more important subject, was also a sealed book at this period of my life; but I gradually assembled much of what was striking and picturesque in historical narrative, and when, in riper years, I attended more to the deduction of general principles, I was furnished with a powerful host of examples, in illustrations of them. I was, in short, like an ignorant gamester, who kept a good hand until he knew how to play it.[34]

The Waverley Novels could be described in precisely that way, the illustration of the principles of historic change by the example of living people involved in it. The powerful host of examples came from Scott's insatiable reading and the collection in his memory of personal reminiscences; the principles from the ideas of the Enlightenment which were all around him as a student in Edinburgh, in conversations with his friends, in the debates of societies like the Literary and the Speculative, in which he played a very active part, and in the lectures, especially those of David Hume. Arthur Melville Clark is too modest about the contribution of the University of Edinburgh to Scott's development:

He learned none of his mighty magic within its walls; and in all the essentials of his art he was . . . self-educated.[35]

This is because Clark sees Scott purely as a romantic; but, as I think is apparent from Scott's own account he needed the catalyst of the Enlightenment ideas. It may have been David Hume's lectures on Scots law which first gave him a glimmering of how he should play his hand.

NOTES

Chapter quotation: Walter Scott, *Ashesteil Memoir.*
[1] **Lockhart, J. G.,** *Life,* Vol. I, Chapter I, p. 29.
[2] *Journal* (18th December 1825), p. 56.
[3] Waverley Novels, Vol. I, p. v.
[4] ibid, p. v.
[5] **Lockhart, J. G.,** *Life,* Vol. I, Chapter 1, pp. 29-30.
[6] Waverley Novels, Vol. I, p. vii.
[7] op cit, Vol. I, p. 31.
[8] Arthur Melville Clark has a useful discussion about Scott's knowledge of these two languages in his book, *Sir Walter Scott: The Formative Years* (1969); on Gaelic, pp. 216-220, and on Norse, pp. 220-221.
[9] **Lockhart, J. G.,** *Life,* Vol. I, Chapter 1, pp. 29 and 35.
[10] Waverley Novels, Vol. 1, p. vii.
[11] **Lockhart, J. G.,** *Life,* Vol. V, Chapter LXXXIII, p. 408.
[12] See, for example, the opening paragraph of Chapter 16 of *The Heart of Midlothian,* Waverley Novels, Vol. 12, p. 277.
[13] *Bicentenary Essays,* p. 294.
[14] **Lockhart, J. G.,** *Life,* Vol. I, Chapter 1, p. 31.
[15] ibid, p. 38.
[16] **Lockhart, J. G.,** *Life,* Vol. I, Chapter 5, p. 128.
[17] **Welsh, Alexander,** *The Hero of the Waverley Novels,* pp. 82-83 (Yale, 1963).
[18] **Scott, Sir Walter,** *Marmion,* Canto IV, Stanza XXX (O.S.A.), p. 135.
[19] **Daiches, David,** *The Paradox of Scottish Culture: The Eighteenth-Century Experience,* p. 71 (London, 1964).
[20] **Lockhart, J. G.,** *Life,* Vol. I, Chapter 1, p. 44.
[21] ibid, p. 46.
[22] *Journal,* p. 670.
[23] **Lockhart, J. G.,** *Peter's Letters to His Kinsfolk,* Ed. by W. Ruddick, p. 66 (Edinburgh, 1977).
[24] **Cameron, The Hon. Lord,** 'Scott and the Community of Intellect' in *Edinburgh in the Age of Reason,* Ed. by George Bruce, pp. 53 and 57 (Edinburgh, 1967).
[25] Quoted in *Bicentenary Essays,* p. 17, from Richard Pares, 'A Quarter of a Millennium of Anglo-Scottish Union' in *The Historian's Business and Other Essays,* p. 89 (Oxford, 1961).
[26] **Cockburn, Henry,** *Journal,* Vol. I, p. 112 (Edinburgh, 1874).
[27] Waverley Novels, Vol. 4, pp. 100 and 124.

[28] **Lockhart, J. G.,** *Peter's Letters*, p. 65.
[29] **Lockhart, J. G.,** *Life*, Vol. III, Chapter XLI, p. 187.
[30] **Thompson, H. W.,** *A Scottish Man of Feeling*, p. 35 (Oxford, 1931).
[31] **Lockhart, J. G.,** *Life*, Vol. I, Chapter 1, p. 33.
[32] **Cockburn, Henry,** *Memorials of His Time*, p. 22 (Edition of 1872).
[33] **Lockhart, J. G.,** *Life*, Vol. I, Chapter 1, p. 45.
[34] ibid, p. 29.
[35] op cit, p. 284.

6

The Enlightenment

'This is the historical Age and this the historical Nation'

In 1821, Scott wrote a series of Prefaces for Ballantyne's *Novelist's Library* and said this about Henry Mackenzie: 'It is enough to say here, that Mr Mackenzie survives, venerable and venerated, as the last link of the chain which connects the Scottish literature of the present age with the period when there were giants in the land – the days of Robertson, and Hume, and Smith, and Home, and Clerk, and Ferguson'[1] – almost the same group as Pleydell's notes of introduction to the circle perhaps at no period equalled 'for depth and variety of talent', the literati, the philosophers and the scientists of Enlightenment Edinburgh. Henry Mackenzie was born in 1745 and died in 1831 and therefore lived from the year of the Jacobite Rising to just before the Reform Bill, or from a time when David Hume was at the height of his power to the year before the death of Scott. Mackenzie was a close friend of both. Certainly then he linked the two ages but in fact one shaded imperceptibly into the other and Henry Mackenzie was by no means Scott's only link with the great age of the giants. In 1819 he wrote to congratulate Lockhart on his book *Peter's Letters to His Kinsfolk*, an account of the contemporary Scottish scene, and said this:

> What an acquisition it would have been to our general information to have had such a work written I do not say fifty, but even five-and-twenty years ago; and how much of grave and gay might then have been preserved, as it were, in amber, which have now mouldered away. When I think that at an age not much younger than yours I knew Black, Ferguson, Robertson, Erskine, Adam Smith, John Home, etc.,

etc., and at least saw Burns, I can appreciate better than anyone the value of a work which, like this, would have handed them down to posterity in their living colours.[2]

We have already seen how the John Home of *Douglas* was attentive to the Scott party in Bath and how Scott read an essay before Principal Robertson, the historian. There were many such familiar and domestic links. David Douglas (the heir of Adam Smith), William Clerk of the Clerks of Pennycuick family, and the younger Adam Ferguson (the son of the author of *An Essay on the History of Civil Society*), were all friends of Scott from his schooldays onwards. Amyat's remark about Edinburgh in its greatest age is often quoted, 'here I stand at what is called the *Cross of Edinburgh*, and can, in a few minutes, take fifty men of learning and genius by the hand'. What he then goes on to say is less familiar. 'In London, in Paris, and other large cities of Europe, though they contain many literary men, the access to them is difficult; and even after that is obtained, the conversation is for some time, shy and constrained. In Edinburgh, the access of men of parts is not only easy, but their conversation and the communication of their knowledge are at once imported to intelligent strangers with the utmost liberality.'[3] It is the same point that Scott makes in talking of Pleydell's introductions: 'a circle never closed against strangers of sense and information'. Not even it seems to boys of fifteen, because Scott was no older than that when he saw Burns in the house of Adam Ferguson in 1787. Although 'several gentlemen of literary reputation',[4] including Dugald Stewart, were present, only Scott chanced to remember, as he modestly put it, the source of some lines of verse which caught the attention of Burns, who rewarded him with a 'look and a word'. The point of the story is that it shows Scott, barely out of school, already moving in the literary circles of Edinburgh.

Some of the giants survived well into Scott's own lifetime. Adam Smith died in 1790 and Adam Ferguson not until 1816, when Scott described him as 'my learned and venerated friend . . . whom I have known and looked up to for thirty years and upward'.[5] I think that it is fair to conclude that there is no gulf, hardly an interval, between the age of the Enlightenment and Scott's own, and that he grew up in this accessible and open community where he could hardly fail to absorb its ideas and attitudes.

The achievements of this remarkable age were, of course, very diverse; they included the geology of James Hutton, the chemistry of Joseph Black, the anatomy of the Monros, and the steam engine of James Watt. But, with the exception of Black, all the men that Scott mentions belong to a distinctive and important strand of Scottish eighteenth-century thought. They were historians and philosophers or 'philosophical' historians. By and large, they shared certain views about the nature of society and historical change which had been developed in Scotland with some influence from Montesquieu. They were views of far-reaching consequence because modern economics and sociology, Marxist theory and the Marxist approach to history were all to some extent derived from them. Adam Smith was the main originator of these ideas, probably as early as 1748 to 1751 when he lectured in Edinburgh. They were developed by Adam Ferguson in *An Essay on the History of Civil Society* (1767) by Robertson in his *History of Scotland* (1759) and in the introduction to his *Charles V* (1769), by John Millar in the *Origin of Ranks* (1771) and innumerable other books over a period of some sixty or seventy years, more or less coinciding with Scott's own life-time. Scott's professors at Edinburgh included several, in addition to David Hume, whose lectures were strongly marked by this sociological or philosophical approach to history, Dugald Stewart, John Bruce and A. F. Tytler. John Bruce left for London, but the others stayed in Edinburgh and were among Scott's friends. Discussions in the Speculative Society in Scott's day revolved round the themes associated with 'philosophical history'. Cockburn said that the liberal young men in Edinburgh at that time lived on the ideas of Adam Smith. 'With Hume, Robertson, Millar, Montesquieu, Ferguson and De Lolme, he supplied them with most of their mental food.'[6] Scott was no Whig, but he enjoyed the company of men like Cockburn and Jeffrey and was associated with them as a contributor to the early numbers of the *Edinburgh Review*.

The general doctrine of this school of history was to see the development of society as a progression from savagery to refinement through several stages, each with a different economic structure. Smith distinguished four of these, hunting and fishing, pastoral, agricultural and commercial. Progress from one stage to another was spontaneous, but not necessarily peaceful, the virtually accidental result of men planning, working and struggling for other things. The stage which man had reached at any particular period largely determined his way of life, his ideas and his institutions. There was nothing final or irreversible about this process because mankind had several times achieved a high degree of refinement only to return to savagery or barbarism. Nor was progress an unmixed blessing. The change from agricultural to commercial society, for example, meant the loss of the kind of community in which man was most content, and the introduction of 'sordid habits and mercenary dispositions', the exaltation of the few and the depression of the many, condemned to mechanical labour which degraded them because it needed no mental effort'.[7] This approach to history, therefore, involved an attitude to the general question of the nature of man and his place in society. It was determinist in the sense that it saw human affairs decided more by impersonal forces than by individual choice and subject to irresistible pressures for change. It was an attitude of 'muted optimism',[8] because it saw that these inevitable changes brought disadvantages as well as benefit.

'I believe this is the historical Age and this the historical Nation' David Hume wrote to his publisher, William Strahan, in August 1770 and went on to say that he knew of no less than eight histories then being written in Scotland.[9] What was the reason for this great outburst of interest in history, amounting almost to an obsession, in eighteenth-century Scotland? Almost everything was approached in a historical spirit. 'Pray, Mr MacQuedy,' said Dr Falliott in Peacock's *Crotchet Castle*, 'how is it all gentlemen of your nation begin everything they write with the "infancy of Society"?'[10] and Sydney Smith: 'The Scotch, whatever other talents they may have, may never condense; they always begin a few days before the flood, and come *gradually* down to the reign of George the Third'.[11] It is generally thought that it had something to do with the Union of the Scottish and English Parliaments in 1707. The loss of national independence was a traumatic shock to which different people reacted in different ways. Some were drawn to history (indeed some still are) because it was only in the historical past that a Scotland 'proud and independent', in Scott's phrase,[12] still existed. Others may have sought in history an explanation of what had happened to help them to come to terms with it. Others again saw the Union as one of several drastic events which made the process of historical change obvious and inescapable. The defeat of the Jacobites at Culloden in 1746 and the suppression which followed caused the abrupt destruction of an ancient way of life. The industrial revolution was transforming society. 'There is no European nation, which, within the course of half a century, or little more, has undergone so complete a change as this Kingdom of Scotland', wrote Scott in the last chapter of *Waverley*.[13]

Against this background it is easy to see why Smith, Ferguson and the other philosophical historians, and Scott himself, should have,taken a view of history that had deterministic and pessimistic overtones. The philosophical historians generally advanced their case by theorising which was closely argued but abstract. It was left to Scott, and this was his great contribution not only to the historical novel but to the writing of history altogether, to give it flesh and bones. Thomas Carlyle was one of the first to remark upon it. He wrote in the *London and Westminster Review* in 1838: '. . . these Historical Novels have taught all men this truth, which looks like a truism, till so taught: that the bygone ages of the world were actually filled by living men not by protocols, state-papers, controversies and abstractions of men. . . . History will henceforth have to take thought of it.'[14] Scott himself made the point more modestly in the passage from the Ashesteil *Memoir* mentioned above,[15] when he speaks about illustrating the general principles of the philosophy of history from the powerful host of examples stored in his mind. It is true that he wrote this at Ashesteil in 1808, and that the first novel, *Waverley*, was not published until 1814; but the first seven chapters were written in 1805, also at Ashesteil. This seems to me a very clear statement indeed that it was the philosophical historians who first revealed to Scott that history was not a disjointed and haphazard series of events, but could be shown to have a pattern and significance, and that they suggested, in a sense, the general theme of the novels.

It is strange that this very clear hint about the importance of the philosophical historians to Scott seems to have been almost entirely ignored until Duncan Forbes drew attention to it in 1953.[16] I say almost because Walter Bagehot had noticed an affinity between Scott and Adam Smith. He was writing about Macaulay and mentions 'his Scotch intellect, which is a curious matter to explain'. He goes on to explain it in these words:

> It may be thought that Adam Smith had little in common with Sir Walter Scott. Sir Walter was always making fun of him; telling odd tales

of his abstraction and singularity; not obscurely hinting, that a man who could hardly put on his own coat and certainly could not buy his own dinner, was scarcely fit to decide on the proper course of industry and the mercantile dealings of nations. Yet, when Sir Walter's own works come to be closely examined, they will be found to contain a good deal of political economy of a certain sort – and not a very bad sort. Any one who will study his description of the Highland clans in *Waverley*; his observation on the industrial side (if so it is to be called) of the Border life; his plans for dealing with the poor of his own time, – will be struck not only with a plain sagacity, which we could equal in England, but with the digested accuracy and theoretical completeness which they show. You might cut paragraphs, even from his lighter writings, which would be thought acute in the *Wealth of Nations*. There appears to be in the genius of the Scotch people – fostered, no doubt, by the abstract metaphysical education of their Universities, but also, by way of natural taste, supporting that education, and rendering it possible and popular – a power of reducing human actions to formulae or principles.[17]

But even after the essay of Duncan Forbes, some critics still confuse the issue by referring to the non-romantic, rational element in Scott as 'Augustan'.[18] This is one of the distortions which results from looking at Scott with English terms of reference in mind. Some of Scott's diverse interests and tastes can be described as Augustan, his liking for Johnson's *Vanity of Human Wishes*, for example; but this is quite a minor matter in comparison to the pervasive influence of the Scottish Enlightenment. A. O. J. Cockshut in his brilliant book on Scott sees that he is not Augustan, but fails to see the full implications of his affinity with the Scottish philosophical historians. He recognises that, for Scott, history (and the main theme in his own writing) was the clash of cultures and that the dichotomy between Rousseau's noble savage and the Augustan view of civilisation was an oversimplification. Cockshut thinks that this means that 'to an extraordinary extent Scott here stands outside the current debate of his time and of the generation before'.[19] This is only true if you look at the intellectual history of the eighteenth century in exclusively English and French terms and ignore everything that had been written in Scotland. Again, Cockshut describes Scott as 'emancipated both from the revolutionary myth of progress and the Augustan myth of finality',[20] but this is because Scott takes the Scottish philosophical view that progress was a mixed blessing and that human affairs are subject to a continuous process of change. 'Unaugustan, too,' says Cockshut is Scott's 'grasp of the irrational as an analysable factor in human affairs'.[21] It may be unaugustan, but it was not un-Scottish. Rational as this philosophy was in its methods, it was under no illusion about the limitations of reason as a guide to human behaviour. 'Reason' in Hume's famous phrase, 'is and ought only to be the slave of the passions, and can never pretend to any other office than to serve and obey them'.[22]

The Augustan idea brings in another red herring. Did Scott subscribe to the view that human nature was unchangeable, that 'Nature and Passion' as Johnson said in the tenth chapter of *Rasselas* 'are always the same'? This was an Augustan commonplace; Pope and Gibbon 'always speak as if human nature was everywhere the same'.[23] Twice at least Scott seems to subscribe to it. In the 'Dedicatory Epistle' to *Ivanhoe*, he speaks about 'the large proportion of manners and sentiments which are common to us and to our ancestors'[24] and in the first chapter of *Waverley* he refers to 'those passions common to men in all stages of society'.[25] Both rather qualified statements, it seems to me, and who would deny that some passions, feelings and instincts change very little from one period to another? A great deal has been written on this subject, and sometimes, as in Devlin[26] or Brown,[27] the issue is further obscured because the idea is described as an 'Enlightenment view'. The unchangeability of human nature was certainly not a view which was consistent with the Scottish 'philosophical' approach to history or with Scott's own ideas as expressed in the novels themselves. They constantly illustrate the way in which human attitudes and behaviour, 'manners', in the way in which the word was then used, change with historical circumstances. It is one of their essential qualities. Cockshut put the point very well:

> Scott was fond in his books set in the seventeenth and eighteenth centuries of shifting the time by about a generation. Thus *Old Mortality* is set in 1679, *Rob Roy* in 1715, *The Heart of Midlothian* in 1736, *Redgauntlet* in about 1770, and *The Antiquary* near the turn of the century, in the days of Scott's own manhood. This enables him to show, in a way that only the imperceptive could thereafter ignore, that a given pyschological type is different in different circumstances. The active fanaticism of Balfour of Burley will develop into the pessimistic stoic

endurance of David Deans. The unselfconscious Highland traditionalism of Rob Roy will become another thing when in the person of Fergus Mac-Ivor it has had time to receive an admixture of French cynicism. The mean, commercial spirit of Morton's uncle in *Old Mortality* is an alien in the old, heroic world; but it will come into its own a generation later in the person of Bailie Nicol Jarvie. The efficient ruthlessness of Grahame of Claverhouse, touched already with a well-disciplined romanticism, will be transposed, three whole generations later, into Redgauntlet's matchless devotion to defeat and despair. For Scott the whole class system is in a state of change throughout the seventeenth and eighteenth centuries; seeing this is one of his most unaugustan insights.[28]

Again 'unaugustan', but, I can only repeat, entirely consistent with, indeed an essential part of, the Scottish 'philosophical' idea of history.

Scott could not have chosen a more appropriate subject for his first novel than the Jacobite Rising of 1745. Not only did it give him a chance to express his Jacobite sympathies and to use his first-hand accounts of eye-witnesses, it was also a perfect opportunity to display the philosophical view of history. Here was a society at one of its decisive moments of change from one 'stage' to another, from a tribal, agricultural community led by chiefs, to Hanoverian commercialism manipulated by the middle-class through Parliament. For a diversity of technological, social and, above all, economic reasons, Highland society was bound to be defeated, so that there was an element of inevitability and determinism about the outcome. As the passionate Jacobite, Flora MacIvor, said when it was all over: 'it was impossible it could end otherwise than thus'.[29] It was progress in a sense, but progress which meant loss as well as gain. Scott wrote of the Jacobites in the last chapter of *Waverley*:

> This race has now almost entirely vanished from the land, and with it, doubtless, much absurd political prejudice; but also, many living examples of singular and disinterested attachment to the principles of loyalty which they received from their fathers, and of old Scottish faith, hospitality, worth and honour.[30]

Adam Ferguson was a Highlander. When he wrote in *An Essay on the History of Civil Society* about the virtues of primitive society and the corruptions of commercialism, he had in mind precisely the same event as Scott, but he expressed his ideas in entirely abstract terms; he never even mentioned the Highlands by name. Scott's account is specific, three dimensional, and expressed through the experience of people, but the underlying ideas are the same.

There is another way in which there is a very strong similarity between the views of Scott and those of the philosophers of the Scottish Enlightenment. They all believed in benevolence. 'Nothing,' wrote David Hume, 'can bestow more merit on any human creature than the sentiment of benevolence in an eminent degree.'[31] By and large, they believed that the majority of people were well disposed towards one another most of the time. Adam Ferguson, in particular, combined his relatively pessimistic view of historical progress with an optimistic view of human nature. *An Essay on the History of Civil Society* is full of remarks like 'love and compassion are the most powerful principles in the human breast' or 'even in the case of those to whom we do not habitually wish any positive good, we are still averse to be the instruments of harm'.[32] Scott was conspicuously generous and benevolent in his own behaviour, and, it seems to me, this sort of attitude illuminates the novels and is one of their greatest charms. There are villains, certainly, usually melodramatic and improbable – like Rashleigh Osbaldistone or Dousterswivel – but the general atmosphere is as optimistic in its expectations of human behaviour as Adam Ferguson.

Even in incidentals, Scott tends to quote Ferguson consciously or unconsciously. There is a passage in the *Essay:* '. . . the human mind could not suffer more from a contempt of letters, than it does from the false importance which is given to literature, as a business for life, not as a help to our conduct, and the means of forming a character that may be happy in itself, and useful to mankind'.[33] Possibly no one has ever written more, or read more, than Scott, but he was fond of echoing Ferguson's words. In the Introduction to *The Lay of the Last Minstrel*, for instance, he said that he avoided confining himself to literary society to 'escape the besetting sin of listening to language, which, from one motive or another, is apt to ascribe a very undue degree of consequence to literary pursuits, as if they were, indeed, the business, rather than the amusement, of life'.[34] There was a sense in which Scott believed this, in spite of the hours which he spent at his desk; but it seems to me that the repetition of the thought, and almost the words, of Ferguson on a point of this kind shows how deeply he was influenced by the attitudes of the 'giants' of the generation immediately before his own.

There is the other important point noticed by R. D. S. Jack, Scott's involvement with the general European tradition, which is apparent in his innumerable references to Cervantes and Ariosto and the like and in the European setting of novels like *Quentin Durward* and *Anne of Geierstein*. 'Scotland necessarily has a prime place in Scott's novels, as he is a Scot and most intimately acquainted with it,' Jack writes, 'but his aim seems to be to relate Scotland and its contribution to the general pattern of European achievement. . . . Properly, he is the literary equivalent of Hume and the eighteenth-century philosophers, making his (necessarily Scottish) contribution to European art'.[35] These philosophers were not only aware of the contemporary European audience, which was one of the reasons why they studiously avoided Scottish particularity and wrote in English as a language of wide currency; they consciously sought the universal. Scott, too, was responsive to European influence and had a European-wide audience; but he made a virtue of Scottish particularity.

NOTES

Chapter quotation: David Hume, *Letters*, Ed. by J. Y. T. Greig (Oxford, 1932), Vol. II, p. 230.

[1] **Scott, Sir Walter,** *The Lives of Novelists* (Everyman's Library Edition, 1928), pp. 294-5.

[2] **Lockhart, J. G.,** *Life*, Vol. III, Chapter XLV, pp. 303-4.

[3] **Smellie, William,** *Literary and Characteristical Lives of Gregory, Kames, Hume and Smith,* pp. 161-2 (Edinburgh, 1800).

[4] **Lockhart, J. G.,** *Life*, Vol. I, Chapter V, p. 115.

[5] *Letters*, Ed. by H. J. C. Grierson (London, 1933), Vol. IV, p. 181.

[6] **Cockburn, Henry,** Memoirs, (Edition of 1872) pp. 39-40.

[7] **Ferguson, Adam,** *An Essay on the History of Civil Society* (1767), pp. 254, 182, 184 (Edinburgh (paperback edition), 1978).

[8] The phrase is Peter Garside's in a very useful essay on this subject, 'Scott and the "Philosophical" Historians', in *The Journal of the History of Ideas*, Vol. XXXVI (1975).

[9] **Hume, David,** *Letters*, Ed. by J. Y. T. Greig, Vol. II, p. 230 (Oxford, 1932).

[10] Quoted by Duncan Forbes in ' "Scientific" Whiggism: Adam Smith and John Millar' in the *Cambridge Journal* (1954), p. 647.

[11] Quoted by Peter Garside, op cit, p. 510.
[12] **Scott, Sir Walter,** Introduction to *Minstrelsy of the Scottish Border.*
[13] Waverley Novels, Vol. 2, p. 416.
[14] *Critical Heritage,* p. 367.
[15] See Chapter 5, p. 55, Note 34.
[16] In his essay, 'The Rationalism of Sir Walter Scott' in *The Cambridge Journal* (Oct. 1953), Vol. VII, pp. 20-35.
[17] **Bagehot, Walter,** *Collected Works,* pp. 416-419 (1965).
[18] Boris Ford, for example (see Chapter 2, p. 12, Note 12).
[19] **Cockshut, A. O. J.,** *The Achievement of Walter Scott,* p. 61 (New York, 1969).
[20] ibid, p. 80.
[21] ibid, p. 80.
[22] **Hume, David,** *A Treatise of Human Nature,* Ed. by I. A. Selby-Biggs, p. 415 (Oxford, 1978).
[23] **Cockshut, A. O. J.,** op cit, p. 77.
[24] **Scott, Sir Walter,** *The Preface to the Waverley Novels,* Ed. by M. A. Weinstein, p. 34 (Nebraska, 1978).
[25] Waverley Novels, Vol. 1, p. 13.
[26] **Devlin, D. D.,** *The Author of Waverley,* p. 46 (London, 1971).
[27] **Brown, David,** *Walter Scott and the Historical Imagination,* p. 179 (London, 1979).
[28] **Cockshut, A. O. J.,** op cit, p. 80.
[29] Waverley Novels, Vol. 2, p. 382.
[30] ibid, p. 417.
[31] **Hume, David,** *Philosophical Works,* Vol. IV, p. 179. See E. C. Mossner, *Life of David Hume,* p. 608 (2nd Edition, Oxford, 1980).
[32] **Ferguson, Adam,** op cit, pp. 35-36.
[33] ibid, p. 31.
[34] O.S.A., p. 51.
[35] **Jack, R. D. S.,** 'Scott and Italy' in *Bicentenary Essays,* p. 294.

7

The Consequences of the Union

'A Kingdom, once proud and independent'

Although Scott often indulged in autobiography, in various passages scattered around in his introductions as well as in the Ashesteil *Memoir* and the *Journal*, he was also reticent about some things. He seldom revealed emotion and he seldom discussed the underlying motives and objectives of his writing. On the few occasions when he does either, there is nearly always a connection with his deep misgivings over the consequence of the Treaty of Union, the erosion of the distinctive characteristics of Scotland. The emotion and the motive appeared together in the Introduction to his first substantial work, *The Minstrelsy of the Scottish Border* (1802):

> By such efforts, feeble as they are, I may contribute something to the history of my native country, the peculiar features of whose manners and character are daily melting and dissolving into those of her sister and ally. And, trivial as may appear such an offering to the Manes of a Kingdom, once proud and independent, I hang it upon her altar with a mixture of feeling which I shall not attempt to describe.[1]

'There is not mistaking,' as Edwin Muir rightly says, 'the emotion in these words.'[2] The same emotion appears in the story which Lockhart tells about Scott's reaction to a meeting of the Faculty of Advocates in 1806 when proposals for some changes in the administration of justice were discussed. Scott opposed them with 'a flow and energy of eloquence for which those who knew him best had been quite unprepared'. Lockhart goes on:

> When the meeting broke up, he walked across the Mound on his way to Castle Street, between Mr Jeffrey and another of his reforming friends, who complimented him on the rhetorical powers he had been displaying, and would willingly have treated the subject-matter of the discussion playfully. But his feeling had been moved to an extent far beyond their apprehension: he exclaimed, "No, no – 'tis no laughing matter; little by little, whatever your wishes may be, you will destroy and undermine, until nothing of what makes Scotland Scotland shall remain." And so saying, he turned round to conceal his agitation – but not until Mr Jeffrey saw tears gushing down his cheek – resting his head until he recovered himself on the wall of the Mound. Seldom, if ever, in his more advanced age, did any feelings obtain such mastery.[3]

The patriotic or nationalist impulse in Scott was obviously very strong. In the words of Lockhart which I have quoted already, 'the love of his country became indeed a passion'.[4] When Scott met Allan Cunningham in 1820 he praised his ballads and 'urged him to try some work of more consequence, quoting Burns':[5]

> That I for poor auld Scotland's sake
> Some useful plan, or book could make,
>   Or sing a song at least[6]

Scott's collection of ballads, like Burns's work on the songs and the anthologies of James Watson and Allan Ramsay at the beginning of the century, was a patriotic endeavour, an act of defence against the threats to the Scottish identity. It is significant, as Daiches has pointed out, that Watson brought out his first volume in 1706 in the middle of the debate on the Union.[7]

There were moments, at least, when Scott was deeply pessimistic about the outcome. In the last paragraph of *Waverley*, he talked about 'the task of tracing the evanescent manners of his own country',[8] and in the Preface to *The Tales of a Grandfather* he said that the 'last shades of national difference may be almost said to have disappeared'.[9] Possibly this is a result of Scott's acceptance of the ideas of the 'philosophical' historians with their doctrine of change that was not intended nor desired but was irresistible. I think that Scott sometimes had the melancholy thought that the complete loss of the Scottish identity by absorption in England was, in the last resort, inevitable. He hated the idea; but, with his customary realism

70

and courage, he tried to accept it. The parallel with *Redgauntlet* is obvious. Was the defence of the Scottish identity as hopeless as Redgauntlet's Jacobitism? Was one a symbol of the other?

Jacobitism and the defence of Scottish independence were, of course, connected historically. In *The Tales of a Grandfather* Scott pointed out that the unpopularity of the Union was one of the main causes of the Jacobite Rising: ' "Prosperity to Scotland, and no Union", is the favourite inscription to be found on Scottish sword blades betwixt 1707 and 1746.'[10] In the last chapter of *Waverley* he described the Jacobites (and, as we have seen, he frequently said that he was one himself) as a 'party, which, averse to intermingle with the English, or adopt their customs, long continued to pride themselves upon maintaining ancient Scottish manners and customs'.[11] Scott, however, was too good a historian ever to oversimplify to the point of suggesting that the two things, the Scottish cause and Jacobitism, were identical. He knew very well that the prevalent mood in Scotland at the relevant time was Whig, Presbyterian and egalitarian and could not accept a cause which was inevitably associated with Catholicism, Episcopalianism and arbitrary royal power. It was this confusion of issues which, as much as anything, led to the Union and made Jacobitism ultimately irrelevant.

Hugh MacDiarmid blamed Scott's novels for 'the paralysing ideology of defeatism in Scotland, the spread of which is responsible at once for acceptance of the Union and the low standard of nineteenth-century Scots literature'.[12] I suppose it can be said that the final chapter of *Redgauntlet* – 'the cause is lost for ever' – does give a sort of nobility to the resigned acceptance of defeat. Did Scott intend this to apply to more than Jacobitism? It is true, as Daiches says of Redgauntlet's character, that 'his zeal is not only for the restoration of the Stuarts; it is, in some vague way, for the restoration of an independent Scotland, and his dominant emotion is Scottish nationalism rather than royalism. Scott made him a symbol of all that the old, independent Scotland stood for, and that is why his fate was of so much concern to his creator. No reader can mistake the passion'.[13] I think that there is indeed a sense of loss about the final scene of *Redgauntlet* that goes beyond the outworn dynastic question and echoes Scott's feelings about the erosion of the 'kingdom once proud and independent'.

71

On the other hand, a year or two after the publication of the novel, Scott in the *Malachi Letters* was stirring up a spirit of Scottish resistance that was anything but defeatist. MacDiarmid in fact saw, as remarkably few people have, that Scott's resistance to anglicisation, the purpose of much of his work but most explicitly so in these *Letters*, 'leads on naturally to the separatist position'.[14] It is not so much Scott himself as his interpreters that MacDiarmid blames for the spread of defeatism, and he includes such people as John Buchan, Herbert Grierson and Edwin Muir. As I shall have cause to mention, there is no doubt that Scott's position on this whole complex of questions has often been misrepresented. Much of this is no doubt ordinary human error. With anyone who wrote as much as Scott, it is only too easy to be misled by a chance remark which may be quite untypical. At the same time, some of the comment on this subject shows an unfortunate tendency to rush to a conclusion without paying much attention to the evidence.

This sort of haste is more often than not applied to the passage in the General Preface to the *magnum opus* edition of the novels where Scott refers to Maria Edgeworth and then describes his own objectives. It is worth quoting in full:

Two circumstances, in particular, recalled my recollection of the mislaid manuscript. The first was the extended and well-merited fame of Miss Edgeworth, whose Irish characters have gone so far to make the English familiar with the character of their gay and kindhearted neighbours of Ireland, that she may be truly said to have done more towards completing the Union, than perhaps all the legislative enactments by which it has been followed up.

Without being so presumptuous as to hope to emulate the rich humour, pathetic tenderness, and admirable tact, which pervade the works of my accomplished friend, I felt that something might be attempted for my own country, of the same kind with that which Miss Edgeworth so fortunately achieved for Ireland – something which might introduce her natives to those of the sister kingdom, in a more favourable light than they had been placed hitherto, and tend to procure sympathy for their virtues and indulgence for their foibles. I thought also, that much of what I wanted in talent, might be made up by the intimate acquaintance with the subject which I could lay claim to possess, as having travelled through most parts of Scotland, both Highland and Lowland; having been familiar with the elder, as well as more modern race; and having had from my infancy free and unrestrained communication with all ranks of my countrymen, from the Scottish peer to the Scottish ploughman. Such ideas often occurred to me, and constituted an ambitious branch of my theory, however far short I may have fallen of it in practice.

Duncan Forbes was referring to this passage when he wrote: '*Waverley* for instance, besides promoting sound morality, was to do for England and Scotland what Maria Edgeworth's Irish Tales had done for England and Ireland: to cement the Union in the hearts of men.'[16] Many other writers have summarised Scott's remarks in a very similar way. Now, it is possible to suppose, if there was no other evidence, that Scott meant to suggest something of this kind, but it is not what he says. Using his knowledge of Scottish characters to show them in a more favourable light than hitherto is not the same thing as 'completing' or 'cementing' the Union.

What, in fact, was Scott's attitude to the Union? There are people who tell us, usually without any supporting evidence, that Scott supported it whole-heartedly. Lord Trevor-Roper, for instance, said once that Scott 'believed passionately in the Union with England. He was a British patriot'.[17] A case can be made for the second of these two statements, but not for the first. Once or twice Scott did express acceptance of the Union, but his acceptance was always reluctant, grudging and conditional. There is no sign in all his writing, or in the reminiscences of his contemporaries, which suggests enthusiasm or passionate belief. In July 1825, he wrote to Maria Edgeworth: 'Dublin is splendid beyond my utmost expectations. I can go round its walls and number its palaces until I am grilled almost into a fever. They tell me the city is desolate, of which I can see no appearance, but the deprivation caused by the retreat of the most noble and most opulent inhabitants must be felt in a manner a stranger cannot conceive. As Trinculo says when the bottle was lost in the pool, "there is not only dishonour in it but an infinite loss". It is a loss however, which time will make good, if I may judge from what I have heard old people say of Edin^r after 1707, which removed the crown from our Israel, – an event which, had I lived in that day, I would have resigned my life to have prevented, but, which, being done before my day, I am sensible was a wise scheme.'[18] That is the most he ever said in favour of the Union, and it is a rather back-handed approval.

The impression which this letter gives accords exactly with the testimony of Lockhart. He never says that Scott had a good word for the Union. On the contrary, he says that Scott, 'ever sensitively jealous as to the interference of English statesmen with the internal affairs of his native kingdom', wrote the *Malachi Letters* (to which I shall come in a minute) 'with as much zeal as he could have displayed against the Union had he lived in the days of Queen Anne'.[19] In a later passage he adds, 'Whenever Scotland could be considered as standing separate on any question from the rest of the empire, he was not only apt, but eager to embrace the opportunity of again rehoisting, as it were, the old signal of national independence'.[20] He goes on to make the somewhat cryptic, if not inconsistent, remark, that Scott would have opposed an 'Anti-English faction, civil or religious' if one had sprung up in his lifetime.[21] Is resisting English interference not, to some degree, anti-English? But perhaps Lockhart was thinking here of a resort to violence on the Irish model, to which Scott was certainly opposed.

As Scott confessed in his letter to Maria Edgeworth, he was inclined to accept the *status quo*. To some extent, this is an attitude which follows logically from the determinist implications of 'philosophical' history. With Scott, it was reinforced by an instinctive conservatism, stimulated by the fear of revolutionary France. His reading of history suggested to him that civilisation was a precarious creation which depended for its survival on the established social pattern, and could be destroyed by violent, abrupt or ill-considered change. Edwin Muir says that Scott 'was a man to whom the established order was sacred'.[22] This is too strong and Lockhart's phrase, 'though an anti-revolutionist, was certainly anything but an anti-reformer'[23] is nearer the truth. Still Scott's instinct was to try to accept what was there, even when it was something he disliked, such as the Treaty of Union.

It would be wrong to draw any conclusions about Scott's own views from remarks by the characters in the novels, especially because of his habit of scrupulous impartiality. Even so, they are worth quoting, for their own sake, as examples of Scott's ability to condense a whole political or economic argument into a sentence or two. It is perhaps significant that in the whole of the *Waverley Novels* there is, as far as I have been able to find, only one remark in favour of what Andrew Fairservice called 'the sad and sorrowful Union',[24] or, as Scott referred to it in the Introduction to *Rob Roy* 'that most obnoxious of measures – the Union of the Kingdoms'.[25] The exception is Bailie Nichol Jarvie's well-known reference to the temporary advantage of access to the tobacco and sugar trade:

'Whisht, sir! – whisht! it's ill-scraped tongues like yours, that make mischief atween neighbourhoods and nations. There's naething sae gude on this side o' time but it might hae been better, and that may be said o' the Union. Nane were keener against it than the Glasgow folk, wi' their rabblings and their risings, and their mobs, as they ca' them now-a-days. But it's an ill wind blaws naebody gude – Let ilka ane roose the ford as they find it – I say, Let Glasgow flourish! whilk is judiciously and elegantly putten round the town's arms, by way of by-word. Now, since St Mungo catched herrings in the Clyde, what was ever like to gar us flourish like the sugar and tobacco-trade? Will any body tell me that, and grumble at the treaty that opened us a road west-awa' yonder?' [26]

Remarks on the other side are fairly frequent, such as Andrew Fairservice's reply to the Bailie:

'That it was an unco change to hae Scotland's laws made in England, and that, for his share, he wadna for a' the herring-barrels in Glasgow, and a' the tobacco-casks to boot, hae gien up the riding o' the Scots Parliament, or sent awa' our crown, and our sword, and our sceptre, and Mons Meg, to be keepit by thae English pock-puddings in the Tower o' Lunnon. What wad Sir William Wallace, or auld Davie Lindsay, hae said to the Union, or them that made it?'[27]

Or Grizel Damahoy in *The Heart of Midlothian* (following Mrs Howden, whom I have quoted already):

'Weary on Lunnon, and a' that e'er came out o't!' said Miss Grizel Damahoy, an ancient seamstress; 'they hae taen awa our parliament, and they hae oppressed our trade.'[28]

Wandering Willie says in *Redgauntlet*:

'Sir John and his father never gree'd weel. Sir John had been bred an advocate, and afterwards sat in the last Scots Parliament and voted for the Union, having gotten, it was thought, a rug of the compensations [share of the bribes] – if his father could have come out of his grave he would have brained him for it on his awn hearthstone.'[29]

Or Redgauntlet himself:

'. . . that wretched pettifogging being, which they still continue to call in derision by the once respectable name of a Scottish Advocate; one of those mongrel things, that must creep to learn the ultimate decision of his causes to the bar of a foreign Court, instead of pleading before the independent and august Parliament of his own native kingdom.'[30]

Some reflections of Scott's views on the Union appears in the biography of Defoe which he wrote for Ballantyne's *Novelist Library*:

De Foe appears to have been no great favourite in Scotland . . . it is not wonderful that, where almost the whole nation was decidedly averse to the union, a character like De Foe, sent thither to promote it by all means, direct and indirect, should be regarded with dislike, and even exposed to the damage of assassination. . . . It is believed that his services were rewarded by a pension from Queen Anne.[31]

The two books where Scott's views on the Union are expressed most explicitly were written at about the same time and towards the end of his life, *The Tales of a Grandfather* (1827) and the *Letters of Malachi Malagrowther on the Proposed Change of Currency* (1826). David Daiches has suggested that where Scott 'thought he stood' on this question might be deduced from the opening chapter of the *Tales*, even if 'it is grossly unfair to reduce the attitude to his country of a great historical novelist to a simplified statement written for a child'.[32] He quotes:

Now as these two nations live in the different ends of the same island, and are separated by large and stormy seas from all other parts of the world, it seems natural that they should have been friendly to each other, and that they should have lived as one people under the same government. Accordingly about two hundred years ago, the King of Scotland becoming King of England . . . the two nations have ever since then been joined in one great kingdom, which is called Great Britain.

But before this happy union of England and Scotland, there were many long, cruel, and bloody wars between the two nations; and far from helping or assisting each other, as became good neighbours and friends, they did each other all the harm and injury that they possibly could by invading each other's territories, killing their subjects, burning their towns, and taking their wives and children prisoners. This lasted for many hundred years; and I am about to tell you the reason why the land was so divided. . . .

But both England and Scotland are now part of the same kingdom, and there is no use in asking which is the best country, or has the bravest men.[33]

Daiches does not comment on the chapters about the Union much further on in the book. As Scott progressed in the *Tales*, he soon abandoned the attempt to write in simplified language, being persuaded that children 'hate books which are written *down* to their capacity'.[34] By the time he reached the events leading to the Union, he was writing in a vigorous robust and realistic manner. In fact, his account of these events long remained the frankest available narrative and the bluntest corrective to the 'Whig' historians, who tried hard to represent the whole sordid business as an unsullied act of wise statesmanship. If Scott's account is blunt and honest, it is not dispassionate; the strength of his feelings is apparent in the force, rhythm and alliteration of his language. The Scots, he says, were desirous of a 'federative union', under which 'Scotland should retain her rights as a separate kingdom, making as heretofore her own laws, and adopting her own public measures, uncontrolled by the domination of England. . . .' The English 'saw, or thought they saw, a mode of bringing under subjection a nation which had been an old enemy and a troublesome friend; and they, very impolitically, were more desirous to subdue Scotland than to reconcile her. In this point the English statesmen committed a gross error, though rendered perhaps inevitable by the temper and prejudices of the nation'. 'These Scottish commissioners, or a large part of them, had unhappily negotiated so well for themselves, that they lost all right of interfering on the part of their country. . . . The distribution of this money constituted the charm by which refractory Scottish members were reconciled to the Union. . . . The feelings of national pride were inflamed by those of national prejudice and resentment. The Scottish people complained that they were not only required to surrender their public rights but to yield them up to the very nation who had been malevolent to them in all respects; who had been their constant enemies during a thousand years of almost continual war. . . . The interests of Scotland were considerably neglected in the treaty of Union; and in consequence, the nation instead of regarding it as an identification of the interests of both kingdoms, considered it as a total surrender of their independence, by their false and corrupted statesmen, . . . despised by the English and detested

77

by their own country.'[35] And so on for more than thirty pages. If after all this, Scott assures the reader that the eventual effect of the Treaty, after about sixty years, was to lead to a 'happy change from discord to friendship – from war to peace, and from poverty and distress to national prosperity'[36] – it hardly eradicates the clear message that he regarded the Union as deplorable and shameful, and as an obstacle to sound relations between the two countries. No one who reads these three chapters – they are Nos. 60, 61 and 62 – is likely to dissent from Daiches's conclusion in his essay of 1951 that Scott 'in his heart had never really reconciled himself to the Union of 1707 (though he never dared say so, not even in his novels)'.[37]

The *Letters from Malachi Malagrowther on the Proposed Change of Currency*[38] were three long letters sent to the Editor of the *Edinburgh Weekly Journal* in February and March 1826 and afterwards published as a pamphlet. It was the only time that Scott used his pen to intervene in a current political controversy, and the letters are the most sustained statement of his political philosophy. It is sometimes suggested that they were on a trivial subject, the right of the Scottish banks to issue their own notes. This right might now be merely symbolic; but it was vital in 1826, when the notes were the only form of currency and credit in Scotland. In any case, as Scott wrote to Robert Dundas – and as is obvious from the *Letters* themselves – he 'desired to make a strong impression, and speak out, not on the Currency Question alone, but on the treatment of Scotland generally', which had been disturbing him for years.[39] He had a 'deep consciousness that there is a duty to be discharged'.[40]

The impulse behind this late work of Scott is the same as that which described in the Introduction to the *Minstrelsy* at the beginning of his career, the desire to protect the Scottish identity against erosion and anglicisation. The *Letters* are a sustained protest against 'a gradual and progressive system' on the part of England to assume control of Scottish affairs, against 'that sort of tutelage to which England seems disposed to reduce her sister country'.[41] There was no advantage to anyone in this practice of handing decisions to 'the tender care of men who know nothing of our country, its wants and its capabilities'. On the contrary, there was already too much centralisation in London: 'that great metropolis is already a head too bulky for the empire. There was virtue in diversity. 'For God's sake, Sir, let us remain as Nature made us, Englishmen, Irishmen, and

Scotchmen, with something like the impress of our several countries upon each.'[42] It was a powerful argument against uniformity and centralisation, and in favour of national diversity and government responsive to local needs and wishes. It is an argument which leads logically to the case for Home Rule.

I note in passing that T. S. Eliot in his *Notes towards the Definition of Culture* (1948) echoes the words of Malachi:

> . . . it is to the advantage of England that the Welsh should continue to be Welsh, the Scots Scots and the Irish Irish. . . . There may be some advantage to other peoples in the English continuing to be English. . . . If the other cultures of the British Isles were wholly superseded by English culture, English culture would disappear too.[43]

A flat uniformity would be the end of all of us. Scott's view a hundred years earlier was precisely the same.

But part of Scott's ingenuity in the *Letters* is to use the Treaty of Union as itself an argument to support his assertion of Scottish individuality. For the Treaty had a positive as well as a negative side; it abolished the Scottish Parliament, but it did give certain guarantees in exchange. One of these guarantees was that no alteration be made on laws which concern private right, '*excepting for the evident utility of the Subjects within Scotland*'.[44] 'We ought not to be surprised,' Scott says, 'that English statesmen, and Englishmen in general, are not altogether aware of the extent of the Scottish privileges, or that they do not remember, with the same accuracy as ourselves, that we have a system of laws peculiar to us, secured by treaties'.[45] He hoped that 'an international league of such importance' would still be found binding on both parties.[46] As far as the currency measure was concerned, 'no advantage, evident or remote, has ever been hinted at, so far as Scotland is concerned: it has only been said, that it will be advantageous to England, to whose measures Scotland must be conformable, as a matter of course, though in the teeth of the articles stipulated by our Commissioners, and acceded to by those of England, at the time of the Union. I have therefore gained my cause in any fair Court'.[47]

At the beginning of the first *Letter*, Scott argued that this policy of interference in Scottish affairs was something quite new. For the first century or so after the Union, Scotland had been left to her own devices, 'under the guardianship of her own institutions, to win her

79

silent way to national wealth and consequence. . . . But neglected as she was, and perhaps *because* she was neglected, Scotland had increased her prosperity in a ratio more than five times greater than that of England'.[48] As so often happens, in matters of Scottish history, modern scholarship confirms that Scott was right. Alexander Murdoch, for instance, who has made a study of Scottish administration from 1707 to 1748, concludes that in this period 'Scotland enjoyed a state of semi-independence' which 'allowed the Union settlement to work by providing a buffer between English government and assumptions, and Scottish institutions and society in general'.[49] This is precisely in accord with Scott's argument in the *Malachi Letters*, which is that the Union would be tolerable as long as England respected the guarantees in the Treaty and left Scotland to run her own affairs in her own way. He could hardly have foreseen the vast increase in Government activity in the nineteenth century against which the Treaty was a completely inadequate defence.

On the immediate issue of the currency, the *Malachi Letters* scored a complete success. They rapidly went through several editions. Public meetings to discuss and endorse their arguments were held all over Scotland and from them a flood of petitions descended on Parliament. In the face of this the Government, within a matter of weeks, withdrew the proposals as far as they affected Scotland. 'The Victory,' as a contemporary writer said 'rested with the author of *Waverley*'.[50] Political pamphleteering has seldom, if ever, secured such a rapid and satisfying result.

In spite of this, and in spite of the importance of the *Letters* both in the history of political thought in Scotland and for an understanding of Scott's own attitudes, they have been largely ignored ever since the initial furore. Literary critics and historians who mention them quite often give the impression of knowing nothing about the *Letters* or of the circumstances in which they were written. Other people who have evidently read the *Letters* misinterpret them in strange ways. Donald Low, for instance, says this:

> The tone of the *Letters* is that of affronted nationalism and political frustration. Yet these powerful feelings are indulged over a subject of limited significance – disagreement as to whether Scottish banks be allowed to issue their own bank-notes. Aggressive emotion is diverted from political actuality to an almost irrelevant area of play.[51]

As we have seen, the bank-note question was not unimportant or divorced from political actuality in 1826, and Scott, far from limiting the discussion, deliberately widened it to include the whole question of the relationship between Scotland and England.

N. T. Phillipson takes a similar line to Donald Low but pushes it ever further: 'Scott', he concludes, 'showed Scotsmen how to express their nationalism, by focusing their confused national emotions upon inessentials. . . . By validating the making of a fuss about nothing, Scott gave to middle class Scotsmen and to Scottish nationalism an ideology – an ideology of noisy inaction'.[52] In using the *Malachi Letters* to argue towards this conclusion, Phillipson misquotes outrageously. Scott begins his argument on the import-ance of the safeguards in the Treaty of Union, to which he returns more than once, by a bitter and ironic passage in which he suggests that the Treaty had been forgotten. In the course of this, Scott says 'even if the old parchment should be voted obsolete'.[53] Phillipson quotes this as 'an old parchment . . . long voted obsolete'.[54] A more glaring example. There is a passage (which I mentioned in Chapter Two) where Scott deplores any idea of the use of force on the Irish model:

> God forbid Scotland should retrograde towards such a state. . . . We do not want to hear her prate of her number of millions of men, and her old military exploits. We had better remain in union with England, even at the risk of becoming a subordinate species of Northumberland, as far as national consequence is concerned, than remedy ourselves by even hinting the possibility of a rupture. But there is no harm in wishing Scotland to have just so much ill-nature, according to her own Proverb, as may keep her good nature from being abused; so much national spirit as may determine her to stand by her own rights, conducting her assertion of them with every feeling of respect and amity towards England.[55]

It seems to me that the meaning of this is absolutely clear. Scott said of the *Letters*: 'I owe my intention regarded the present question much less than to try if it were possible to raise Scotland a little to the scale of consideration from which she has so greatly sunk.'[56] It is obvious from every paragraph that the last thing he wants is to see Scotland running the risk of becoming a subordinate species of Northumberland. But he is also against violence. For him, the one unquestionable advantage of the Union was that it brought peace and an end to the war which had lasted a thousand years. Almost anything was better than a return to the slaughter and destruction. Phillipson, however, renders the passage as follows: 'Indeed, so horrified was he at the thought of a breach of the Union, that he wrote that it would be far better that Scotland should become "an inferior sort of Northumberland" than that the structure of the Union should be harmed.'[57] Distortion could hardly be carried further, except by Trevor-Roper. With his well-known anti-Scottish spleen, he leapt on to this particular band-wagon in an article in *The Times* where he carried the misquotation still further away from its original: 'He (Scott) believed that it would be better for Scotland to be an inferior appendage to Northumberland than to be independent, but that its permanent union with England could be sweetened by converting its deplorable past history into an agreeable romance.'[58]

I have gone into these distortions at some length because there seems to be a fairly wide-spread myth that Scott was an uncritical enthusiast for the Union. Such ideas are often repeated without any supporting evidence or argument, almost as though it were a deliberate propaganda campaign. The Phillipson myth, insubstantial as it is, is already taken seriously by people who are unaware that it rests on such frail and false foundations.

Some of Phillipson's points are sound enough and do not need the support of misquotation. It is perfectly true, as he says, that Scott 'had no faith in the Union as an obstacle to the Government'.[59] Who did? Scott knew perfectly well, and said so at some length in *The Tales of a Grandfather*, that the ink was hardly dry on the Treaty before the English majority in Parliament began to disregard its provisions whenever it suited them. Scott's appeal to the Treaty was a debating tactic, a delaying action designed to slow down the advance of anglicisation; but he knew that it was going to be a long and hard struggle. He said as much in his *Journal*:

> The consequence will in time be, that the Scottish Supreme Court will be in effect situated in London. Then down fall – as national objects of respect and veneration – the Scottish Bench, the Scottish Bar, the Scottish Law herself, and – there is an end of an auld sang. Were I as I have been, I would fight knee-deep in blood ere I came to that. But it is a catastrophe which the great course of events brings daily nearer. . . . I

82

shall always be proud of *Malachi* as having headed back the Southron, as helped to do so, in one instance at least.[60]

It is true, of course, that Scott did not take the next step which follows logically from the *Malachi Letters*, the advocacy of Home Rule. That he did regard himself as struggling for the cause of Scottish independence appears from the letter to Sir Robert Dundas on 9th March 1826[61] from which I have already quoted: 'I think that John Hume mentions that Hepburn of Keith, a private gentleman of pleasant manners and high accomplishments, was regretted by the Whigs as having induced him to sacrifice himself to a vain idea of independence of Scotland. With less to sacrifice and much fewer to regret me, I have made the sacrifice probably as vainly. But I am strongly impressed with the necessity of the case.' Scott was in fact living in the middle of the only period since the Union when Home Rule was not a conceivable policy. Gordon Donaldson has distinguished three periods in the history of the Scottish attitude to the Union.[62] The first, which lasted to about 1750 was one when the Union was very unpopular and there was a strong desire to see the end of it. From about 1750 to 1850 the Union 'went almost unchallenged'; it was 'part of the established and unalterable order of things'.[63] Then from about 1850 onwards, the Union has come increasingly under challenge and more and more specific proposals have been advanced for Scottish independence.

Why was it seen as unalterable in Scott's own day? It was partly because the Union had been so unobtrusive during most of the eighteenth century. Scotland was, in practice, largely self-governing anyway. When James Stuart Mackenzie was appointed in 1761 to take over the management of such Scottish affairs as the Government in London handled, he was surprised to find no papers in his office and no sign that any business was being carried on.[64] It was a period when Scotland was advancing in prosperity, not necessarily because of the Union, but at least in spite of it. With an unreformed House of Commons, any popular agitation against the Union would simply have been disregarded, or suppressed as treasonable if it became troublesome enough. The bloody reprisals which followed the '45 were not a very distant memory, and there was an association in the official, as well as the popular, mind between Jacobitism and the assertion of Scottish independence. For all these reasons, the prevailing fashion in the Edinburgh of the Enlightenment was to make the best of the bad job by accepting, even encouraging, assimilation. It is apparent from their letters that men like David Hume were consciously Scottish, and proud of it, but they did their best in their public writings to be as English as possible and even to write as though Scotland did not exist. Scott changed all that, but there were limits. He was realistic and he was in favour of peace and stability. He saw the danger of pressing resistance to the point where it could only produce frustration, bitterness and, perhaps, violence. 'It is difficult to steer betwixt the natural impulse of one's national feelings setting in one direction, and the prudent regard to the interests of the empire and its internal peace and quiet, recommending less vehement expression. I will endeavour to keep sight of both. But were my own interest alone concerned d——n me but I would give it them hot!'[65]

At the same time, Scott also thought that the process of anglicisation which he was resisting was, in itself, unsettling and dangerous. He saw Scottish national feeling as part of the cement which held society together. If it was weakened or destroyed by interference and innovation from England, there would be a vacuum which might be filled by 'democratic' or 'revolutionary' emotions, and for Scott, under the influence of French Revolutionary terror, the two words meant much the same. He expressed the thought in his *Journal* and in letters to Lockhart and to Crocker,[66] whom the Government had chosen to write the official reply to Malachi. Of the three, the last is the most explicit:

> But Scotland, completely liberalised, as she is in a fair way of being, will be the most dangerous neighbour to England that she has had since 1639. There is yet time to make a stand, for there is yet a great deal of good and genuine feeling left in the country. But if you unscotch us you will find us damned mischievous Englishmen. The restless and yet laborious and constantly watchful character of the people, their desire for speculation in politics, or anything else, only restrained by some proud feelings about their own country, now become antiquated and which late measures will tend much to destroy, will make them, under a wrong direction, the most formal revolutionists who ever took the field of innovation.

Among all the writings of Scott, the *Malachi Letters* were unique. They are not only his only public intervention in political controversy, they are the fullest and most open expression of his strong feelings about Scotland. Against all the forces of character, time and circumstances which pressed for reticence, this was the one occasion when he came close to speaking his real mind. 'I sincerely believe,' wrote Lockhart (who, after all, knew him better than almost anyone else), 'that no circumstances in his literary career gave him so much personal satisfaction as the success of Malachi.'[67] There is a revealing episode in the *Life* of Scott by his contemporary George Allan:

> The Author's own feelings, as we learn from a gentleman then connected with Mr Ballantyne's establishment, were excited in an unusual degree on this occasion. Two days after the first letter had appeared, he was in the printing-house with his friend Mr Ballantyne, when the latter remarked that he had been more solicitous and careful about the proof of this little composition, than he had ever observed him to be respecting any of his productions. 'Yes,' said he, in a tone that electrified even this familiar friend, who had heard him speak before under all varieties of circumstances, 'my former works were for myself, but this – *this is for my country!*'[68]

NOTES

Chapter quotation: Sir Walter Scott, Introduction to *Minstrelsy of the Scottish Border.*
[1] **Scott, Sir Walter,** op cit, Introduction, p. cxxxi.
[2] **Muir, Edwin,** *Scott and Scotland,* p. 137.
[3] **Lockhart, J. G.,** *Life,* Vol. I, Chapter XV, p. 460.
[4] See Chapter 1, Note 37, **Lockhart, J. G.,** *Life,* Vol. V, Chapter LXXXIV, p. 435.
[5] ibid, Vol. III, Chapter XLVIII, p. 374.
[6] **Burns, Robert,** 'The Answer to the Guidwife of Wauchope-House' (1787), O.S.A., p. 261, lines 18-20.
[7] **Daiches, David,** *The Paradox of Scottish Culture,* p. 13 (London, 1964).
[8] Waverley Novels, Vol. 2, p. 420.
[9] **Scott, Sir Walter,** *Tales of a Grandfather,* edition of 1889, Preface, p. XXII.
[10] ibid, p. 771.
[11] Waverley Novels, Vol. 2, p. 417.
[12] **MacDiarmid, Hugh,** *Lucky Poet,* p. 202 (London, 1943).

[13] **Daiches, David,** 'Scott's Achievement as a Novelist' in *Literary Essays,* p. 113 (Edinburgh and London, 1956).

[14] **MacDiarmid, Hugh,** op cit, p. 203.

[15] Waverley Novels, Vol. 1, pp. XII–XIV.

[16] **Forbes, Duncan,** op cit, p. 26.

[17] **Trevor Roper, Hugh,** 'Sir Walter Scott and History', *The Listener,* 19th August 1971, p. 226.

[18] **Scott, Sir Walter,** *Familiar Letters,* Vol. II, pp. 311–12.

[19] **Lockhart, J. G.,** *Life,* Vol. IV, Chapter LXVII, p. 441.

[20] ibid, Vol. V, Chapter LXXXIV, p. 445.

[21] ibid, Vol. V, Chapter LXXXIV, p. 446.

[22] **Muir, Edwin,** op cit, p. 22.

[23] **Lockhart, J. G.,** *Life,* Vol. V, Chapter LXXXIV, p. 446.

[24] Waverley Novels, Vol. 8, pp. 16, 22.

[25] ibid, Vol. 7, p. XXXIX.

[26] ibid, Vol. 8, p. 148.

[27] ibid, Vol. 8, pp. 148–9.

[28] ibid, Vol. 12, p. 57.

[29] ibid, Vol. 35, pp. 174–5.

[30] ibid, Vol. 35, p. 263.

[31] **Scott, Sir Walter,** *Lives of the Novelists,* pp. 361–2 (see Chapter 6, p. 58, Note 1).

[32] *Bicentenary Essays,* p. 59.

[33] **Scott, Sir Walter,** *Tales of a Grandfather,* pp. 2 and 6 (see Chapter 2, p. 15, Note 25).

[34] **Lockhart, J. G.,** *Life,* Vol. V, Chapter LXXIII, p. 112.

[35] **Scott, Sir Walter,** *Tales of a Grandfather,* pp. 749, 768, 754, 770.

[36] ibid, p. 771.

[37] See Note 13, p. 118.

[38] **Scott, P. H.,** 'The Malachi Episode' in *Blackwood's Magazine* of Sept. 1976, pp. 247–61.

[39] **Lockhart, J. G.,** *Life,* Vol. IV, Chapter LXIX, pp. 479–80 and *Letters,* Vol. 9, p. 438.

[40] *Letters,* Vol. 9, p. 465.

[41] *Letters from Malachi Malagrowther,* Scott, *Miscellaneous Prose,* edition of 1847, Vol. 1, p. 747.

[42] ibid, p. 748.

[43] **Eliot, T. S.,** op cit, p. 57.

[44] See Note 41, p. 731.

[45] ibid, p. 739.

[46] ibid, p. 732.

[47] ibid, p. 740.

[48] ibid, p. 726.

[49] **Murdoch, Alexander,** *The People Above*, p. 27 (Edinburgh, 1980).

[50] *The Crocker Papers*, Vol. 1, p. 314.

[51] *Bicentenary Essays*, p. 315.

[52] In 'Nationalism and Ideology' in *Government and Nationalism in Scotland*, Ed. by J. N. Wolfe, p. 186 (Edinburgh, 1969).

[53] See Note 41, p. 732.

[54] **Phillipson, N. T.,** op cit, p. 183.

[55] See Note 41, pp. 727-8.

[56] Scott in *The Arniston Memoirs*, Ed. by G. W. T. Ormand, p. 324 (Edinburgh, 1887).

[57] **Phillipson, N. T.,** op cit, p. 183.

[58] *The Times*, 28th April 1976.

[59] **Phillipson, N. T.,** op cit, p. 183.

[60] *Journal*, p. 208.

[61] See Note No. 56.

[62] **Gordon Donaldson and others,** 'Scottish Devolution: The Historical Background', in title described in Note 52 above, pp. 4-6.

[63] ibid, pp. 4, 5.

[64] **Murdoch, Alexander,** op cit, p. 106.

[65] *Journal*, p. 134.

[66] *Journal*, p. 153, *Letters*, Vol. 9, pp. 465, 471.

[67] **Lockhart, J. G.,** *Life*, Vol. V, Chapter LXXXIV, p. 445.

[68] **Allan, George,** *Life of Sir Walter Scott* (Edinburgh, 1834), p. 478. Scott refers to the same episode in his *Journal* entry for 24th February 1826 (p. 132).

8

Conclusion

'Scotland never owed so much to one man'

Can we now attempt some answers to the questions with which we started, what did Scott owe to Scotland and what Scotland to him? I think that the answer to the first question is, on the surface at least, self-evident. Scott grew up, and spent his life, in a complex of over-lapping and interlocking communities in Scotland. First, there was the community, both real and legendary, of his Border family and associations, seen as continuing the spirit of the Border ballads. Then the High School, an intense 'little republic',[1] devoted to the Romano-Scottish outlook on life, and creating a wide circle of close friends for life. In 1826, forty-three years on, Scott wrote of Lord Melville, 'I could never have lost remembrance of the very early friend with whom I carried my satchel to school, and whose regard I have always considered as one of the happiest circumstances of my life'.[2] He could have said the same of scores of people. Already through these friends he became part of the literary and philosophical society of Edinburgh when he was little more than a schoolboy. The University, both through its lectures and its debating clubs, strengthened these links and these influences. So did his training and career in the law, a bastion of Scottish tradition. The High School, the University, the law, literary and philosophical Edinburgh were all one closely knit group of men, knowing one another with the intimacy that came from living in a town so compact that they were bound to meet almost every day.

Scott had a gift for this friendship and conviviality, but he also had, or thought he had, an instinctive preference for the life of solitary reflection. He said this more than once in his letters and *Journal*, as in this passage:

> Few men, leading a quiet life, and without any strong or highly varied
> change of circumstances, have seen more variety of society than I – few
> have enjoyed it more, or been *bored*, as it is called, less by the company of
> tiresome people. I have rarely, if ever, found any one, out of whom I
> could not extract amusement or edification; and were I obliged to
> account for hints afforded on such occasions, I should make an ample
> deduction from my inventive powers. Still, however, from the earliest
> time I can remember, I preferred the pleasure of being alone to waiting
> for visitors, and have often taken a bannock and a bit of cheese to the
> wood or hill, to avoid dining with company. As I grew from boyhood
> to manhood I saw this would not do; and that to gain a place in men's
> esteem I must mix and bustle with them. Pride and an excitation of
> spirits supplied the real pleasure which others seemed to feel in society,
> and certainly upon many occasions it was real. Still, if the question was,
> eternal company, without the power of retiring within yourself, or
> solitary confinement for life, I should say, 'Turnkey, lock the cell'.[3]

A man of this temperament might easily have retreated from
society, if he had not been, as Scott was all his life, surrounded by
accessible and congenial company. They contributed greatly, as
Scott himself points out, to the content of the novels, where the
characters, incidents and even the dialogue largely derived from the
observations which Scott stored in his extraordinary memory as he
travelled about in Scotland. Similarly, his 'philosophic' approach to
history was formed not only by his reading of Smith and Adam
Ferguson, but on his conversations with them and their successors.
In a very real sense, Scott's work grew out of his daily life in
Edinburgh and the Borders. His poetry was most effective when, as
in *Proud Maisie*, for instance, it was closest to the feel of the Border
ballads, just as his best novels as those set in the Scotland that he
knew intimately. 'No Scotchman of his time' as Thomas Carlyle
said, 'was more entirely Scotch than Walter Scott: the good and the
not good, which all Scotchmen inherit, ran through every fibre of
him.'[4]

As we have seen, Scott often mentioned the foreign influences on
his work, particularly Cervantes and Ariosto. Many of these, the
German romantic dramatists, the early Italian poets and the rest,
were probably what Scott had in mind when he talked about the

'nonsensical' trash 'with which he had stuffed his head'.[5] Certainly when the effect is obvious, especially perhaps that of the English 'Gothick' novelists, it is nearly always unfortunate. The melodramatic paraphernalia in Scott is derived from such sources, and it is quite different in tone from the stark and matter of fact approach to the supernatural where Scott followed the Border ballads. The pasteboard figures in the novels are those that speak a laboured and genteel English. Most of the novels set outside Scotland are unreal and tushery-ridden. To quote Kurt Wittig again, 'Scott usually is greatest when most Scottish'.[6] If we ask what Scott as a writer owes to Scotland then the answer is almost everything, the emotional impulse, the ideas, the characters, the historical situations and their interpretation, the language and the humour.

The argument of Edwin Muir's book, *Scott and Scotland*, as far as it concerns Scott, is that Scotland failed him. It could not help him to come to terms with his 'riotous imagination', because this needed more than the superposition of the 'complexity and exactness' of Scots law. It needed the sort of reconciliation that 'might have been found in a whole body of experience radiating from a centre in an autonomous society'.[7] Scotland, as Muir saw it, was no longer such an 'organic society with its own conventions of thought and sensibility. . . . It was trying to imitate England'[8]; it was 'a broken image of the lost Kingdom'.[9]

Muir's final conclusion was that 'it is of living importance to Scotland that it should maintain and be able to assert its identity'.[10] Ironically enough, he does not seem to realise that Scott would have entirely agreed with him on this point, and that much of his writing was devoted to precisely this purpose. Partly this is because Muir takes the conventional view that Scott quite simply accepted the Union and therefore the inevitable melting of Scottish manners into those of England. Muir does this, I suspect, because he had not read Scott very widely and had taken many of his conceptions uncritically and ready-made. If he had read more, in Scott's *Journal* and *Letters* for example, he could hardly have failed to see that Scott was very much part of a living community which sustained, encouraged and served him at every turn. In Scott's day, Scotland was still very much an 'autonomous society', although one under strong threat, and it was the threat that was the spur to Scott's emotions. Perhaps in this negative sense, the threat served the purpose of stimulating him to write at all. It gave the edge to 'the patriotic enthusiasm', in Lockhart's words, 'which mingled with the best of his literary efforts'.[11]

The central argument in Muir's book is about language. He argued that the Scottish consciousness was divided because Scots had ceased to be a homogeneous language suitable for all purposes. Scots therefore 'feel in one language and think in another', and 'when emotion and thought are separated, emotion becomes irresponsible and thought arid'.[12] Scots therefore tended to be used for simple lyrics because the emotion in one language was not controlled by the thought of the other.[13] There is a good deal of force in this theory, even if it is pushed too far, but it is curious that Muir should have chosen to put it forward in a book about Scott, because the example of Scott tends to undermine the argument. Muir himself towards the end of the book, admits that Scott wrote far better Scots than English and that his dialogue was 'the best Scots prose that has ever been written'. This is a little surprising after what has come before, but Muir rescues consistency by arguing that the Scots was used 'for the simplest purposes of humour and pathos'.[14] I have already said enough about the dialogue in Scots, and it seems clear to me that it not only often expresses deep feeling, but feeling tempered and modified by thought. Divided as the Scottish consciousness was, with linguistic confusion partly as cause and partly as result (for I accept Muir's basic premise), Scottish speech was still vigorous enough in Scott's time at least to give him one of his greatest literary assets.

What, on the other hand, did Scott do for Scotland? I remarked in my first chapter how frequently the word 'gratitude' comes up when people are writing about this in Scott's own day. Another example is in the *Scotsman* of 4th March 1826 in a report of a public meeting held to discuss the banknote question, the immediate pretext for the *Malachi Letters*. 'The gratitude of the country was due to him,' said a speaker, 'if ever gratitude was due to any man.' There was great applause, the newspaper adds, 'all looking towards Sir Walter Scott.' In this case the gratitude was clearly directed to Scott's defence of Scottish rights and interests in the *Malachi Letters*.

Another specific instance of gratitude is mentioned by Lockhart when he is talking about the attitude of Highlanders during the preparations for the visit of George IV: 'No man could have coaxed them into decent co-operation, except him whom all the Highlanders, from the Haughtiest MacIvor to the slyest Callum-beg, agreed in looking up to as the great restorer and blazoner of their traditional glories'.[15] It seems then, that an element in all this is that Scott had succeeded in the objective described in the General Preface to the Waverley Novels of showing the people of Scotland – in this instance the Highlanders – 'in a more favourable light than they had been placed hitherto'.[16] In this Preface, Scott spoke of the English as the audience to whom this demonstration was to be made. (It is consistent with this idea, of course, that the hero-as-passive-observer in several of the novels is an Englishman travelling in Scotland, such as Edward Waverley himself.) Probably the more important result of this aspect of Scott's writing was the internal reconciliation within Scotland between Highlander and Lowlander. It could, I think, be demonstrated that the ancient distrust between the two communities has been almost entirely demolished and almost single-handed by Scott himself. This is not the least of the debts which the country owes to him.

Meadowbank's speech, which I quoted at the end of the first chapter, said that Scott had conferred a new reputation on Scotland. At first glance, this may seem mere after dinner rhetoric when one thinks of the intellectual pre-eminence of the Scotland of David Hume and Adam Smith. It did not require Scott, one might suppose, to rescue Scotland from a comparative obscurity. But there is a curious thing about the writers of the Enlightenment, which I mentioned briefly in the previous chapter. They suffered from a painful inhibition about Scotland. It is often said that Scottish writers reacted to the loss of independence in 1707 in two opposite ways. They either returned demonstratively to older Scottish literary traditions, like Ramsay, Robert Fergusson and Burns; or, like David Hume and Adam Smith, they set about proving that Scotsmen, independence or no independence, could still be in the vanguard of European thought, using English, as a widely acceptable language, more effectively than the English themselves. Since the Union in 1707 was humiliating and shameful, they tried to forget it almost by pretending that Scotland did not exist at all. Some of these writers in some moods at least, almost, as it were, tried to be English.

When David Hume was acting as Embassy Secretary in the

British Embassy in Paris in 1764, Gilbert Elliot of Minto said in a letter to him, 'love the French as much as you will, . . . but above all continue still an Englishman.' Hume replied indignantly: 'I do not believe there is one Englishman in fifty, who, if he heard that I had broke my neck tonight would not be rejoic'd with it. Some hate me because I am not a Tory, some because I am not a Whig, some because I am not a Christian, and all because I am a Scotsman. Can you seriously talk of my continuing an Englishman? Am I, or are you, an Englishman? Will they allow us to be so? Do they not treat with Derision our Pretensions to that Name, and with Hatred our just Pretensions to surpass and to govern them?'[17]

This was the Hume who spoke of the Scots as 'the People most distinguished for literature in Europe',[18] who spoke of the 'Barbarism of England'[19] and expressed surprise to Gibbon that an Englishman of that age could write so distinguished a book as his *Decline and Fall*,[20] and who spoke Scots all his life. But it was the same David Hume who wrote an essay on 'National Character', without mentioning the Scots, and who went to enormous trouble to purge 'Scotticisms' from his writing. He patronised very generously a minor versifier, Thomas Blacklock, who wrote in English; but is not recorded as taking any interest in Robert Fergusson. He was concerned about the controversy over Ossian, but not at all about the genuine Gaelic poetry that was being written in his own day. In all of this, of course, Hume was typical of the Edinburgh literati of the time, men of great clarity of mind in certain directions, but of abject blind spots in others. David Daiches says of them, with appropriately polite moderation, that they had a 'total lack of equipment . . . to deal with a whole area of imaginative literature'.[21] In fact, it was so total that it threatened to destroy, if it had been allowed to prevail, not only all poetry in Scots or Gaelic, but any sort of balanced and complete view of Scotland itself.

I think that it was because Scott saw so clearly where this school would lead, in spite of all its admirable qualities, that he was so pessimistic about the future of Scotland. At the time of the *Malachi* affair, he wrote to Lockhart:

> But my heart will not brook . . . to leave the cause of my country as I do sincerely conceive it to be in a state so precarious without doing whatever one poor voice can to sound the alarm.[22]

Scotland was under attack on two fronts simultaneously, the English tendency to assume control of Scottish affairs, which was the subject of the *Malachi Letters*, and this North British aspiration on the part of the literati to follow through the implications of the Union uncompromisingly. Of the two, it was probably the internal surrender which was the more insidious.

As far as I am aware, Lockhart was the first to notice where Scott stood on this question. He discussed it in some detail in *Peter's Letters to his Kinsfolk*, published in 1819. When he was writing it, he had the benefit of a long conversation with Scott on this very subject. Scott had invited him to Abbotsford when he heard that Lockhart proposed to write about the intellectual and artistic life of Scotland. He said in a letter: 'I want to give you the advantage of some of my experience respecting the state of our Scottish literature about twenty-five years since'.[23] There is an account of this visit to Abbotsford in No. LV of *Peter's Letters,* where Lockhart contrasts Scott's attitude to the Scottish past, and to Scottish feeling, with those of the literati. He begins by noting the use which Scott had made of the Scottish past in his poetry and novels:

> Whatever direction the genius of his countrymen may take in future years, the benefit of his writings must ever be experienced in the great resuscitation of slumbering elements, which they have produced in the national mind. Perhaps the two earliest of his poems, the *Lay of the Last Minstel* and *Marmion*, are the most valuable, because they are the most impregnated with the peculiar spirit of Scottish antiquity. . . .
>
> In like manner, in those prose Tales – which I no more doubt to be his than the poems he has published with his name – in that delightful series of works, which have proved their author to be the nearest kinsman the creative intellect of Shakespeare has ever had – the best are those the interest of which is most directly and historically national – *Waverley* and *Old Mortality*. The whole will go down together, so long as any national character survives in Scotland – and themselves will, I nothing question, prolong the existence of national character there more effectually, than any other stimulus its waning strength is ever likely to meet with.

The Scottish past had been largely ignored before Scott (and here presumably Lockhart has in mind the habit of the literati in their obsession with history to draw their examples from anywhere but Scotland).

The folly of slighting and concealing what remains concealed within herself, is one of the worst and most pernicious that can beset a country, in the situation where Scotland stands. Although, perhaps, it is not now the cue of Scotland to dwell very much on her own past history (which that of England has thrown too much into the shade), yet she should observe what fine things have been made even of this department, by the great genius of whom I have spoken about – and learn to consider her own national character as a mine of intellectual wealth, which remains in a great measure unexplored.

But it was not only the Scottish past which the literati had ignored, but whole areas of poetry and feeling:

The most remarkable literary characters which Scotland produced last century, showed merely (as I have already said) the force of her intellect, as applied to matters of reasoning. The generation of Hume, Smith &c., left matters of feeling very much unexplored, and probably considered Poetry merely as an elegant and tasteful appendage to the other branches of literature, with which they themselves were more conversant. The disquisitions on morals were meant to be the vehicles of ingenious theories – not of convictions of sentiment. They employed, therefore, even in them, only the national intellect, and not the national modes of feeling.

The Scottish literati of the present day have inherited the ideas of these men, and acted upon them in a great measure – with scarcely more than the one splendid exception of Walter Scott. While all the rest were contenting themselves with exercising and displaying their speculative acuteness, this man had the wisdom – whether by the impulse of Nature, or from reflection, I know not – to grapple boldly with the feelings of his countrymen.

And Lockhart concludes:

I consider him, and his countrymen should do so, as having been the sole saviour of all the richer and warmer spirit of literature in Scotland.[24]

He was, as Lockhart described him in an earlier passage, 'the great genius to whom whatever is Scottish in thought, in feeling, or in recollection, owes so large a share of its prolonged, or reanimated, or ennobled existence'.[25]

I have quoted these passages from Lockhart at some length because they have been strangely overlooked in all the voluminous criticism of Scott, and because they reflect, I think, not only Lockhart's impressions but Scott's own idea of his objectives, explained in these long conversations at Abbotsford. Certainly, Scott would have estimated his achievements much more modestly, but there can be no doubt from the whole of Scott's life and writing that his aims were as Lockhart describes them. We have seen how much Scott valued 'the peculiar spirit of Scottish antiquity', that he wished to 'prolong the existence of national character', and add the 'national modes of feeling' to the exercise of the intellect. I think that it is because he did all of this with such triumphant success that his own country responded with the gratitude that Meadowbank, Cockburn and the others describe. In his own day, Scott was afraid that Scotland was about to disappear into the mists of forgotten things. That it has not done so is due more to him than to anyone else. He was more successful than he supposed.

Of course, Scott was not alone. Ramsay, Robert Fergusson and Burns, and the collectors of folk song, had revived and enlarged the Scottish literary tradition at the same time as the literati of the Enlightenment turned their backs on it. Galt's novels were as firmly based as Scott's on the life and language of Scotland. But the impact even of Burns was at first too local, and he could be dismissed as a peasant prodigy. The restoration of national self confidence, and of international awareness and acceptance of Scotland, needed a man of Scott's power to win an audience as wide as the literate world. Perhaps in that class-conscious age it also needed a man who was indubitably a gentleman as well as a genius. To a generation nurtured on a prose literature which ignored Scotland (although this is not quite true of Adam Smith) Scott was a liberation. Scotland, its languages and its people still existed after all, and could be openly acknowledged and celebrated in books read eagerly everywhere. Cockburn in his *Memorials* described the impact in Scotland of the first publication of *Waverley*:

> The unexpected newness of the thing, the profusion of original characters, the Scotch language, Scotch scenery, Scotch men and women, the simplicity of the writing, and the graphic force of the descriptions, all struck us with an electric shock of delight.[26]

Scott had released Scotland from the limbo of the secret places of the mind.

NOTES

Chapter quotation: Henry Cockburn, *Journal*, entry for 22nd September 1832.

[1] Waverley Novels, Vol. 35, p. 6.

[2] **Lockhart, J. G.,** *Life*, Vol. IV, Chapter LXIX, p. 478.

[3] *Journal*, pp. 65–66.

[4] *The Critical Heritage*, p. 353.

[5] *Journal*, p. 56.

[6] **Wittig, Kurt,** *The Scottish Tradition in Literature*, p. 234 (Edinburgh and London, 1958).

[7] **Muir, Edwin,** *Scott and Scotland*, (1936), p. 127.

[8] ibid, p. 132.

[9] ibid, p. 141.

[10] ibid, p. 182.

[11] **Lockhart, J. G.,** *Life*, Vol. 1, Chapter X, p. 297.

[12] **Muir, Edwin,** op cit, p. 21.

[13] ibid, pp. 28–42.

[14] ibid, p. 174.

[15] **Lockhart, J. G.,** *Life*, Vol. IV, Chapter LVI, p. 34.

[16] Waverley Novels, Vol. 1, p. XIII.

[17] **Mossner, E. C.,** *Life of David Hume*, p. 469 (2nd Edition, Oxford, 1980) and *Letters of David Hume*, Ed. by J. Y. T. Greig, Vol. 1, p. 470 (Oxford, 1932).

[18] **Hume, David,** *Letters*, Vol. 1, p. 255.

[19] ibid, Vol. 2, p. 104.

[20] ibid, Vol. 2, p. 309.

[21] **Daiches, David,** *The Paradox of Scottish Culture*, p. 77 (London, 1964).

[22] **Scott, Sir Walter,** *Letters*, Vol. 9, p. 442.

[23] **Scott, Sir Walter,** *Familiar Letters*, Vol. II, p. 40.

[24] **Lockhart, J. G.,** *Peter's Letters to his Kinsfolk*, Ed. by William Ruddick, pp. 143, 146–7, 148 (Edinburgh, 1977).

[25] ibid, p. 132.

[26] **Cockburn, Henry,** *Memorials of His Time*, p. 241 (Edinburgh, 1872).

Selected Bibliography

Works of Walter Scott

Only a very small part of Scott's work is at present in print. Several of the novels, including *Waverley, Guy Mannering, The Antiquary, Old Mortality, Rob Roy, The Heart of Midlothian* and *Redgauntlet* are available in Everyman's Library, or World's Classics, or Penguins. *Selected Poems* are available from Carcanet, but not the full *Poetical Works,* edited by J. Logie Robertson for the Oxford Standard Authors Series. The most recent and accurate edition of the *Journal,* that edited by W. E. K. Anderson (Oxford, 1972) is out of print. James C. Corson's very useful *Notes and Index to Sir Herbert Grierson's Edition of the Letters of Sir Walter Scott* (Oxford, 1979) is available, but not the letters themselves which were published in twelve volumes between 1932 and 1937. There is no available edition of the miscellaneous prose; and the edition of the *Malachi Letters,* which I edited for Blackwood's in 1981 is now out of print.

There have, however, been so many editions and reprints of Scott that copies of at least the novels and poems can be found fairly easily. The *Magnum Opus,* for which Scott wrote additional notes and introductions, has been often reprinted. *The Miscellaneous Prose* was reprinted in a similar format.

The first three volumes of the new *Edinburgh Edition of the Waverley Novels,* (*Kenilworth, Old Mortality* and *The Black Dwarf*) were published in August 1993. The remaining 27 volumes will follow at a rate of two or three each year. This edition goes back to the measurements and printers' proofs to produce a text as close as possible to Scott's intended words.

Biographies

There is a recent, careful and comprehensive biography, *Sir Walter Scott* by Edgar Johnson, in two volumes (Macmillan, 1970). J. G. Lockhart's *Memoirs of Sir Walter Scott*, one of the greatest of biographies, is sometimes inaccurate or biased; but as Scott's son-in-law he had the incomparable advantage of intimate personal knowledge. It is, therefore, quite literally, irreplaceable. There have been many reprints of the full text in several volumes as well as of the one-volume abridgement. Of many modern one-volume biog-raphies, probably the best are: John Buchan: *The Life of Sir Walter Scott* (1932, and several times reprinted) and Sir Herbert Grierson: *Sir Walter Scott, Bart* (1938).

Criticism

Scott, The Critical Heritage, edited by John O. Hayden (London, 1970) is a very convenient anthology of nineteenth-century criticism. Among many recent essays, two are especially important: David Daiches's 'Scott's Achievement as a Novelist' (first published in 1951 and reprinted in *Literary Essays* (1956); and Duncan Forbes's 'The Rationalism of Sir Walter Scott' (*The Cambridge Journal*, Vol. VII, Oct. 1953).

There have been several excellent books on Scott in the last few years, including especially: A. O. J. Cockshut, *The Achievement of Walter Scott* (University Press, New York, 1969); D.D. Devlin, The *Author of Waverley* (Macmillan, 1971); Alan Bell (Editor), *Scott Bicentenary Essays* (Scottish Academic Press, 1973); David Brown, *Walter Scott and the Historical Imagination* (Routledge and Kegan Paul, 1979), A. N. Wilson, *The Laird of Abbotsford: A View of Sir Walter Scott* (Oxford, 1980); Graham McMaster, *Scott and Society* (Cambridge, 1981) and Thomas Crawford, *Walter Scott* (1982); Graham Tulloch's *The Language of Walter Scott* (André Deutsch, 1980) is an illuminating study of Scott's copious and inventive use of words.

SOME SALTIRE PUBLICATIONS

Complete list (and details of the Saltire Society, membership etc.) available from the:
The Saltire Society,
9 Fountain Close,
22 High Street,
Edinburgh EH1 1TF